Decisions

On Making the Right Ones More Often

By Jack Warner

—A Memoir with a Purpose—

Published by
Quatrefoil, Inc.
312 Four Seasons Lane
Montvale, NJ 07645

ISBN: 978-0-9778056-2-4

Everything in the memoir is true and reported honestly, to the best of the Author's recollection. There have been no exaggerations, embellishments, or fictionalizing of any kind. All names, places, locations and companies are real.

For Matthew, Barbara, Peter, and Christopher
and
Patrick, Brendan, Claire, Xavier and Roxy

—With Love—

Decisions

On Making the Right Ones More Often

By Jack Warner

—A Memoir with a Purpose—

DECISIONS

There are hundreds of books on decision-making. This one is different. Because it's an actual case study of a single life, spanning nearly ninety years. And that life is mine...reported here in the form of an annotated memoir.

But before delving into my life story, I'd like to tell you why I wrote this book...and offer you some thoughts about the whole decision-making process.

❖ ❖ ❖ ❖

<u>Why I wrote this book</u>—
When you get old and your career is long behind you...when your children and even your grandchildren are grown with independent lives...when your closest friends have moved away...and most significantly, when your beloved spouse has passed on and you now once more live alone...you can't help but look back to reflect upon your life in full.

And when you do, you see how each of life's major decision points has altered your course. With each decision...whether good or bad or neutral...leading to another decision point.

1

Followed by another, and another, and another...to eventually take you to the place you find yourself today.

So as never before, you grasp the importance of good decision-making. Not just for the "here and now"...but for its long-term impact on your life, and on the lives of others that you love. So you mull over each of your past decisions. How and why you made them...and where you went right or wrong.

You also realize something else. You've probably never shared with your children some of the key events and major turning points in your life. Things you should have told them when they were little, when they were growing up, and when they were leaving home.

So you decide to write your memoirs, in the hope that your children and grandchildren and generations beyond might find them instructive...or at least interesting. (Or at the very least, that your jottings will give them some understanding of what life was like "way back then"...and give them some appreciation of the family heritage from which they've sprung!)

One often hears it said—"That with age comes wisdom." Clearly, that's not always true. But with age comes <u>experience</u>. And that experience leads to <u>insights</u>...which in the very best of cases might qualify as "wisdom".

I certainly don't pretend to be a purveyor of wisdom. But as I reflect back on my life, a number of key insights do come sharply into view. And it seemed a shame not to record them for generations yet to come. Part of an inheritance, if you will. An inheritance of insights and ideas.

It's up to you to decide if they're of any interest or value. But my deepest hope is that you'll find them useful tools in your journey through life.

❖   ❖   ❖   ❖

The Decision-making Process—
In its fullest sense, this is a book about the decision-making process...with the challenge of making the right decisions far more often. Because good decision-making is the key to both longer-term happiness and "a life well lived".

We can't control the future...world events, political and cultural shifts, natural disasters, etc. But we can control our lives. And it's our decision-making that gives us that control!

In the pages that follow, you'll read about some of the pivotal experiences and key decisions that have shaped my life. A mini-autobiography, if you will!

Interspersed among them are reflections on the insights and beliefs that they've generated. In most cases, these insights and beliefs did not come as "epiphanies" or "Eureka Moments". Rather, they've come well after...as an old man, looking back and asking..."how did I get here?...and "what's it all about?"

Then, at the end of this book, I'll try to summarize everything in a list of "life-principles" that have worked for me. And I hope for you!

Jack Warner
Father / Grandfather / Great Grandfather / Friend
December 2024

Life's Journey

My Journey—

Compared to many, my journey through life may seem fairly seamless and straightforward. But looking back, I can now see that circumstance presented me with at least 12 major decision points. And significantly, four of these decision points might never have occurred were it not for the help of a number of Mentors who opened my eyes to greater possibilities.

Of course, I'll never know if taking other paths might have proven wiser. While I'm certainly pleased with all the paths I did take...and where they have led me...that's not the point! Rather, it's reflecting on the decision-making process itself, more so than on the specifics.

We're all different. And your life will be, and should be, quite different than mine. The details of my journey are relevant only because they may help to illustrate the cumulative impact of what might seem at first to be fairly non-consequential decisions. But added together, they can have profound consequences. Life is all about decisions. And as stated, making the right ones is vitally important. And helping you make the right ones more often is my goal with this book.

❖   ❖   ❖   ❖

Your Journey—

To each of us life is a 'journey'...with a series of divergent paths to choose from. Where each junction leads is uncertain. Some have signposts. Others do not. Some lead to dead ends. Others circle back to the beginning. Some take us to places closer to our goal.

Sadly, we don't have a route map or an aerial view. And compounding the problem is that at different stages in life we're likely to reassess the destination we seek.

So how throughout life do we make the best decisions on which paths to follow?

We have three resources to guide us—

1. <u>Our Intuition</u>—based on our own personal experiences and 'gut feel'.
2. <u>The Experience of Others</u>—tapping into the knowledge of those who have traveled these paths before.
3. <u>A Mentor</u>—Simply put…"a wise and loyal personal advisor."

The smart move of course is to take full advantage of all three of these resources. So let me elaborate a bit on each—

❖　❖　❖　❖

1. Intuition—

As we age and grow, we gain personal experience that helps to guide us through life…and helps to keep us from harm. That's a valuable thing!

But as emotional creatures, our critical decision-making can be handicapped. Based on past experience, we may be overly cautious and adverse to risks...or overly daring and actually thrilled by risks...or become so frozen in indecisiveness that we allow chance and circumstance to rule our lives.

So in order to overcome these emotional roadblocks, we would be well advised to go beyond pure intuition in making our important decisions.

2. The Experience of Others—

We study history, not because it will likely repeat itself, but because it lets us see the final outcomes of the personal decisions that others have made in the past. The pitfalls. The successes. The mistakes. The adaptability that turns setbacks into gains.

While the times, places and situations may differ very widely, basic 'human nature' remains pretty much the same. Thus history can provide us with a clear window into the decision-making successes and failures of many who have come before us. We can learn from both positive and negative role models...expanding our own experience many-fold.

Throughout the ages, people of wisdom have stressed the importance of studying the past. To quote just a few—

> *"We are like dwarfs standing upon the shoulders of giants, and so are able to see farther than the ancients"*
> Bernard of Chartres, circa 1130

"Those who cannot remember the past are condemned to repeat it."

George Santayana, 1905

"Those who fail to learn from history are doomed to repeat it"

Winston Churchill 1948

3. **A Mentor**—By definition—"A wise and loyal personal advisor." A number of the world's most successful people have credited a personal Mentor with helping them make many of the key decisions that have led to their success. Those naming their personal Mentors include—Bill Gates, Oprah Winfrey, Mark Zuckerberg, Yves Saint-Laurent, Elon Musk and even Mother Teresa. And there are thousands more.

    But you don't have to be someone of prominence to find and gain help from a Mentor. For most of us, they're right out there in plain sight, willing to help if we just take the effort to seek out their wise counsel. And reaching out to them is one of the most important things a person can do to increase their odds for success.

    So what makes a good Mentor? A true Mentor doesn't make decisions for you, or tell you what to do. Simply by sharing their experience and asking you the right questions, a Mentor opens your eyes to new possibilities and helps you discern for yourself the best paths to achieving your goals. And more than likely, they'll help you rethink and possibly even change your short and long term goals.

A true Mentor is far more than just a sounding board, but obviously he or she has to be a good listener. And vastly important, the Mentor must be non-judgmental. It's <u>their questions</u> that awaken the ideas and solutions that <u>you alone</u> formulate.

Typically, the right Mentor is an older, successful, experienced individual who is willing to share their knowledge and some of their time with a younger person in whom they see some potential. A longer-term relationship is ideal. But even a single lunch or private meeting or two may prove life-changing.

If all this sounds a bit idealized and makes finding the right Mentor seem somewhat beyond reach, don't fret. As you move through life and keep your eyes open, you'll no doubt cross paths with a number of individuals that you admire... individuals who may agree to share a little of their wisdom and time with you. They might not think of themselves as Mentors...but in fact that is what they'll be.

(On a personal note—Through good fortune and a little effort, I've had no fewer than four Mentors at various stages in my life. As you read through this book, you'll learn how I found them and learn the profound effect they had upon me.)

1 + 2 + 3 = More than the sum of the parts—

By combining all three of these personal resources...Intuition, the Experience of Others, and a personal Mentor...the likelihood of your choosing the right paths in life will be significantly increased!

❖ ❖ ❖ ❖

What about Luck?

We call it "Good Luck" to be in the right place at the right time... or by sheer chance to meet the right person. But at the outset, how can you know whether that's going to be "Good Luck" or not? It's only much later...after making and acting upon a series of decisions...that you can look back and call it "Good Luck" or "Bad". Was it an opportunity acted-upon or ignored? Were your expectations realistic? Were your actions sufficient to succeed? Did you plow doggedly ahead when you should have regrouped or moved on?

Good Luck is often defined as "beating the odds". Flip a coin and you have a 1-in-2 chance of winning. Pick a spouse and you have a 1-in-3 chance of a truly happy marriage. Start a new business and you have a 1-in-10 chance of it surviving. Beating those odds requires clear-eyed decision-making...not only at the outset, but at every toss of the coin, bump in the road, or month that goes by.

Someone once said—"You make your own luck." You make it by acute decision-making!

❖ ❖ ❖ ❖

How Far Can You Travel?—

I've always loved analogies because they make abstract concepts more visual and easier to understand. And I can think of few better analogies for life's long journey than the NASA Voyager Space Missions. Voyager successfully probed Jupiter and its moons, and then went on to reach Saturn, Uranus, Neptune and the far reaches of our outer Solar System. This accomplishment amazed me because I hadn't realized that we had rocket propulsion systems anywhere near powerful enough to travel that far. And then I learned...we didn't!

So how did Voyager get us there? It did it by harnessing the gravitational and centrifugal forces of closer planets to effectively "slingshot" us off to the next more distant planet...and by then repeating that process again and again. Obviously, this took enormous planning, accurate targeting, precision timing, and enough blastoff thrust to reach the next planet without being lost in space. But NASA did accomplish all this—taking us to places long thought far beyond our farthest reach.

Now for the analogy—
We travel through life in a series of stages...moving from one stage to the next, with critical decision points at each juncture. Our first stage is 'childhood'...where we orbit around our family and community. Then at some point in time, we elect to 'blast off' and 'slingshot' ourselves to our next stage in life. (Be that to new locations, new relationships, further study, the start of a career, or whatever.) And there we remain...in that new orbit... until we decide to 'slingshot' off again to our third stage in life.

While NASA had a celestial map to guide them, unfortunately we do not. We must rely on 'dead reckoning' to choose our next destination and the precise moment and trajectory and thrust needed to get there. These are critical decisions that deserve all the wisdom we can muster...because a miscalculation could result in one of two things going wrong—

1. If we're indecisive...and take no action or too little action... we could remain forever trapped in a particular stage's orbit, never escaping its gravitational pull. (For some that may be all they really need or want in life. But for others, this may commit them to an unfulfilling life of regret.) Or...
2. If we miscalculate...we could 'slingshot' off in the wrong direction or at the wrong time...and find ourselves forever wandering in space...never finding the secure platform we need for our next jumping-off point.

Of course, there's always the possibility that we may have chosen the wrong target for our next stage in life. It may appear bright and shiny and easily reached...but once we arrive there, we may find that it lacks the atmosphere and gravity necessary to sustain us. (If that is the case, a rapid 'blast off' may be the wise move. Delay will typically only compound the problem!)

<u>To complete the analogy</u>...
We may shoot for the stars...but where we end up in life is largely determined by our success in traveling through a series of stages. Selected wisely, each stage gives us the momentum to reach higher. But we must decide precisely the right moment and right trajectory to successfully reach our next

target. And we do this again and again until we arrive at our final destination.

A 'stage' in this analogy may be a particular position with a certain employer...and the next 'stage' a <u>far more senior</u> position with the same or different employer. Or it might be an entirely new career path, or a new vocation, or starting your own business or practice...close to home or far distant. A 'stage' could even be a person...an accomplished individual around whom you orbit, gaining experience and contacts. But beware—the more fulfilling and rewarding that each 'stage' proves to be (i.e.-the strength of its gravity), the more difficult will be your decision to leave it!

❖ ❖ ❖ ❖

It's all about decisions...
Certainly every life presents us with pivotal decisions. Some easy, some tough. Some that come to us through chance, or circumstance, or opportunity. Some that are brought to us by others. And some that are the products of our own study, planning, and creativity.

Then we act on those decisions, with no real assurance that they'll turn out well. And if they don't, we have some new decisions to make. On and on it goes.
That's life!

❖ ❖ ❖ ❖

Over my lifetime, I've experienced them all. Good decisions and bad. And by sharing my own personal journey in this book, I hope to provide you with some insights that might prove valuable as you chart your own personal course and make your own pivotal decisions…hopefully to the ultimate place you want to be.

So let's begin—

My Childhood

A Slice of Time—

We're all born into a slice of time. And that slice largely determines how we see the world and shapes the values we believe in.

For me, that slice of time began in 1936. The Great Depression had just ended and World War II was soon to begin. As a child I saw that holding a job and stretching your finances were absolute keys to a stable and happy family life. I saw that great evil truly does exist in the world and that major sacrifices were demanded to combat it and survive it. Without question, I lived in a time of the "we" generation that was vastly different than the "me" generation that we have today. And the "we" was family, neighborhood, parish and country. Everything centered around these four.

❖ ❖ ❖ ❖

I can vividly remember the Japanese attack on Pearl Harbor. The seemingly unstoppable Axis conquests of both Europe and Asia. The uncles, cousins and neighbors shipping overseas to fight. The women going to work in war plants and support services. The war posters and movies and bond drives. The Gold Star flags going up in more and more windows across town, signifying that yet another husband or son had died in battle.

I remember the strict rationing of food, gasoline, rubber, and much more. The bans on long-distance travel and long-distance phone calls. And the absolute bans on the sale of new cars and washing machines and other home appliances. I remember planting our Victory Garden, collecting tinfoil, milkweed pods, fat, and scrap metal for the war effort. I remember the Air-Raid Drills and blackouts...going out at night with my father on his rounds as an Air-Raid Warden, to make sure that every window had its blackout curtains drawn and that all outside lights were extinguished until the "All-Clear" sounded. And I can remember...as if yesterday...the radio announcement that something called "The Atomic Bomb" had just been dropped on Japan. And most of all, I remember the joy and excitement as we all took to the streets when first VE Day and then VJ Day finally arrived!

❖ ❖ ❖ ❖

I was born into a time where self-sacrifice, and hard work, and frugality, and patriotism were prized as one's key virtues. A time where family and country always came first. A time where religious devotion was central to American life. There's little doubt that all this has played a major role in shaping my life and my attitudes. So view this as a disclaimer, if you will.

I know that your slice of time will be radically different from mine. But many of the <u>universal principles</u> and <u>underlying yearnings</u> in life still decidedly apply. So hopefully you'll find the details in my life relevant to your own decision-making process. And that you'll gain a greater appreciation of how each major decision in life necessarily leads to another decision, then another, then another, in your long journey.

❖ ❖ ❖ ❖

With all that said—Now, let's travel back in time to my earliest days and my earliest influences… to the very small town where I grew up. Its unusual history. My family. My pals. The things we did. And what life was like for me during my childhood years. In short—those major influences on me <u>before</u> I was old enough to start making my own decisions.

❖　❖　❖　❖

Green Island—

My boyhood home was in the small village of Green Island…a place where the Hudson and Mohawk Rivers converged just west of Troy, NY. The main channel of the Hudson separated us from downtown Troy. But only a narrow, fast-running channel of the Mohawk River separated us from Watervliet and Cohoes and all the other towns to the west. In recent years that channel has been diverted through underground conduits and covered with a roadway. But back in my day, that channel and its large outflow basin proved particularly dangerous. Almost every year or so, one or two kids on skates would break through the winter ice and be swept away beneath the ice pack. While every parent warned of the danger, 'double dares' made skating across it a boyhood challenge to prove your manhood. (But being an obedient kid, I never attempted it.)

I said that Green Island was small. In fact, it still holds the honor of being the smallest town in New York State…just seven-tenths of a square-mile. And that includes the two tiny islands in the mid-Hudson that are officially part of Green Island. They were unoccupied and overgrown in my day, and the smallest still is. We called it 'Monkey Island' and we would walk over to it during low tide to play Tarzan. I'm told it's now called McGill Island. Don't know why.

The larger island was 'Center Island', and it was bisected by a railroad bridge that connected the southern end of our town to downtown Troy. Back in the early 1900s Center Island had a baseball field at its northern end, and a tent-making factory at its southern end. There were no signs of either when I was a kid, just a small, empty, overgrown island. Sometime after I left the area, several large oil storage tanks were built on Center Island's southern half. And much later an apartment complex was built on its northern half. Today, the oil tanks are long gone, replaced by a luxury condo development. To spur sales, they've renamed the place 'Starbuck Island'.

Though living in a pretty small town, we were far from isolated. The center of Troy was directly across the river. And Albany, the State Capital, was only 8-miles south.

❖ ❖ ❖ ❖

When I was a boy, Green Island had a working-class population of about 4,300 and three major employers...a large Ford Motor Company plant that produced car radiators and chassis leaf springs...a Bendix factory that produced automotive brake linings (asbestos in those days)...and a Behr Manning plant (now owned by Norton Abrasives) that produced sandpaper.

Years earlier, Green Island also had a truly amazing railroad coachworks company that created luxury parlor cars for America's power barons and for both European and South American monarchs. Called 'The Gilbert Car Works', it employed at its peak over 800 highly skilled artists, artisans and craftsmen, to create what were acclaimed "unique works-of-art". The company had moved to Green Island in 1853 after a massive fire destroyed their operations in Troy. Before the move, they had specialized in luxury horse drawn stagecoaches. But in Green Island their sole concentration became high-end custom railcars...capitalizing on the country's enormous new wealth and headlong rush to build railroads.

The Gilbert Car Works introduced the world's first Parlor Cars, Sleeping Cars, and Dining Cars. Other companies tried to copy their innovations. But none came close. When unveiled, the press acclaimed their suite of railcars for Don Pedro of Brazil... "A Palace on Wheels". Every detail was called breathtaking. Even the screw heads were gold plated. The Company's railcars for the King of Spain...and for international opera star Adelina Patti...were even more sumptuous. Patti...who always insisted that she be paid in gold...was the highest paid opera singer in both Europe and the Americas. Her suite of Gilbert railcars was commissioned to become her official home on wheels...with a drawing room car, dining car, and sleeping car.

❖   ❖   ❖   ❖

There's a reason why all these major companies built plants in tiny Green Island. Back in 1823, to make the Hudson River navigable north of Troy, a Federal Dam with a Boat Lock was built... stretching across the river from Green Island to Troy. The Dam's spillway had the added benefit of providing the area with a major source of hydraulic power.

Then just two years later, in 1825, the Erie Canal was completed, with its eastern terminus at the mouth of the Mohawk River, just north of Green Island and Troy. The Erie Canal had a profound effect on America's growth...opening up the Country's still sparsely populated interior. By providing a continuous water route from the Port of New York to Lake Superior, shipping and transportation costs were slashed by over 90-percent. Population began to boom in the Midwest...and for the first time, New York City became America's principal seaport. The Erie Canal made New York the 'Empire State'.

And the singular place where the Erie Canal and the Hudson River joined together? The Troy/Green Island area!

Soon the area's waterfronts were bustling with barges, side-wheeled steamships, and sloops. And the Nation's first two railroad lines crossed and connected at a point just west of Troy. Seizing upon this burgeoning opportunity for profits, hundreds of manufacturers, entrepreneurs and tradesmen flocked to the area...transforming Troy into a booming industrial city. And before long, that prosperity and opportunity was extended to Green Island, with the 1835 construction of a 1,600-foot railroad drawbridge spanning the Hudson. Before then, the River could be crossed only by boat or by ice-sled when the Hudson was frozen.

By the end of the century, Troy had become the fourth wealthiest city in America., with hundreds of magnificent homes and dozens of showcase public buildings. Nightlife was lively...but as a 'port city', somewhat bawdy.

Meanwhile, Green Island's growth was strictly industrial.

One of the first major businesses on the Island was the 'George Tibbets Sawmill', built in 1836. Each day until the winter freeze, thousands of logs...cut down and harvested in the Adirondacks... were floated down the Hudson to fulfill the Country's growing demand for lumber. With a prime location just above the Federal Dam, the Tibbets Sawmill soon became the Nation's largest sawmill. That same year, the 'Troy Airtight Stove Company' built a plant in Green Island to meet the burgeoning demand for wood burning cooking stoves in the Midwest. Several other companies soon followed, building plants on the Island.

One particularly notable event occurred in August 1919, when a caravan of 50 cars arrived in Green Island to set up a riverside campsite for four important friends—Henry Ford, Thomas Edison, Harvey Firestone, and the naturalist John Burroughs. Edison had picked the spot, which was not far from his main plant in Schenectady. While there primarily for leisure and good fellowship, Henry Ford immediately recognized the potential of the Federal Dam as a source of electrical power... which led to his decision to build a major Ford Motor Company plant in Green Island. The plant opened in 1923, and at its peak employed over 1,000 workers.

❖   ❖   ❖   ❖

Of course, all that's somewhat lost to history. When I was a kid, all those Green Island glory days were never even mentioned at home or in grade school. In the late 1930s and early 1940s, we were just a quiet, small, fairly poor working-class town that had struggled through the Great Depression...and that was now coping with the enormous challenges of World War II. We were just ordinary simple folks. Nothing special. But looking back, I now realize that I was surrounded by some very special people. Kind and very decent people. People with a strong work ethic. People with unbridled patriotism. People who almost never complained. People with what we would call today... 'strong family values'.

❖   ❖   ❖   ❖

Our home was a small 2-bedroom bungalow at 53 Arch Street... modest at 960-sq. ft.—but one of the nicest in town. Our back yard opened onto a very large lot where we played Cowboys and Indians and built forts. A few blocks beyond that was the undeveloped northern half of the Island. Everyone called it 'The Prairie" and we'd frequently explore it or fish off its fairly high riverbanks. So living in Green Island was like living in the country...while being just minutes away from a good size city with all that city life had to offer. Though in truth, Troy had somewhat faded from its glory days only 30 or 40 years before. Still, Troy was fairly prosperous, with a lively downtown area bristling with department stores, shops, restaurants, and three movie theatres. It was also home to RPI (Rensselaer Polytechnic

Institute) and Russell Sage College. But as industries would continue to move south over the next 30 or so years, Troy's decline would become severe. However, all that has now reversed... with high tech industries making Troy once again a place to be!

❖   ❖   ❖   ❖

But back to the 1930s and 1940s...
and the specifics of my story—
I was the only living child of George and Anna Warner. I say "living" because a daughter, Joan, was born to my parents some years earlier. But due to complications, she lived for less than an hour. Even though warned that another pregnancy might prove fatal, at age 35 my parents brought me into the world on March 26, 1936.

When I was much much older, they told me that the final days before my birth had proved especially worrisome. Two weeks before her due date, my mother in a dizzy spell fell down the concrete steps at the back door, breaking her right arm. Then three days before my birth, they learned that a major flood was on the way. Heavy rains and melting ice were causing the Hudson River floodgates to breach. Within hours, Green Island was inundated and cut off. The floodwaters rose to 26-feet before calming. Arch Street was awash right up to the southeast corner of our house. The bridge to Troy was closed and weighted down with loaded railcars to keep it from floating off its piers. What to do? Two valiant firemen came to my parents rescue, rowing them across the Hudson, where a driver took them to the Troy Hospital for my delivery the next day.

Little wonder that my parents showered me with love through-out all of their lives! Which in my father's case was all too short. He died at 58 from ALS...amyotrophic lateral sclerosis... perhaps better known as Lou Gehrig's Disease. My mother, who everyone called Ann rather than Anna, remained a widow until her death just shy of 102. And for all that time, in her eyes I could do no wrong.

My maternal grandparents...Joe and Rita Teson lived right next door, in a house identical to ours. They were both French and both first generation Americans. My grandfather told me that his father came from Paris, where he was a walking stick maker. My grandmother said her father was from Strasbourg in the Alsace region, where he was a schoolteacher. Her maiden name was Shaver. They could speak French, but never did so with me.

Both my Teson grandparents were born in 1876 and always lived in Green Island. I'm told that my widowed great-grand-mother Shaver ran a boarding house there, and that when she died, her 16-year-old daughter...my grandmother Rita...had to take over. Young Rita was somewhat overwhelmed by the responsibility. So when her beau Joseph Leo Teson (who was also 16) proposed that they be married...and that together they could keep the place going...she enthusiastically said "Yes". They ran the boarding house for several years.

Grandpa Joe was a warm and joyful man, much loved in Green Island. People called him "The Rose of Green Island" because as a teenager he always had a fresh or silk rose fastened to his buggy pole. While still in his teens, he learned the steam boiler

27

building trade and worked as a 'boiler maker' at the *D&H Railroad Steam Locomotive Works* in Cohoes. In his early thirties, he was elected to the Green Island Village Board and served as Police Commissioner. After the Great Depression, he worked for New York State at the steam-generating power plant in Albany, which supplied both heat and electricity to all the surrounding State office buildings.

Grandma Rita was reserved and a bit formal...not one to hug you or act playful. She had no siblings as far as I know.

Grandpa Joe's mother was still alive and living in Green Island when I was very young. She lived with an Uncle Vic a few blocks away. He was a barber and I'm not sure how he was related. Her son-in-law, I think? She spoke only French and we all πcalled her Mémé-Mère...which is French for "Our Mother". When she died, several relatives came down from Montreal to join in her 3-day wake at Vic's house. As was their custom, the women all gathered respectfully in the parlor, while the men convened raucously in the kitchen. Even though I was just six, they included me. As the wine flowed, the stories and laughter grew to dizzying levels. You could say this was 'my coming of age'. Certainly, it was the best time I had ever had up to that point in my young life! They may talk about 'Irish Wakes' and 'Italian Wakes'...but there's nothing like a 'French-Canadian Wake'. At least not this one!

❖ ❖ ❖ ❖

<u>My mother...Anna Frances Warner</u>...was the middle of three children born to Joe and Rita Teson. The oldest was my Aunt Irene. She lived in Troy and was the widow of Tommy Flynn who had died while still very young. They had just one daughter...my cousin Joan Ann. Many years later, Aunt Irene married Harold Peasley who was a retired railroad engineer. Cousin Joan Ann married Everett Rugg when she was 18 and they moved to Buffalo. Some years later she remarried and became Mrs. Lyman "Dusty" Rhodes. Joan outlived both of her husbands and died in 2022 at age 88. She had two daughters...Sharon Rugg Moak and Linda Rugg Rozany...and several grandchildren and great-grandchildren.

Aunt Irene was a live wire, playing the piano, singing, and performing as Carmen Miranda in local Church shows. As a young girl, she played piano in one of Troy's larger movie theaters, adding excitement and romance to their silent films. Diphtheria as a child had left Aunt Irene somewhat deaf. So to compensate, she spoke very loudly and had to wear an old-style hearing aid that hung in a big pouch from her neck.

My mother's younger brother...my Uncle Joseph...was married to Rose Simmons when they were both 16. They lived in Watervliet, an industrial town just west of Green Island. They had a son and a daughter...my cousins Bobby and Lorraine. When young, my Uncle Joseph was a very popular semipro baseball player who everyone called...Joe Teso. They assumed he was Italian like his wife's family, rather than French. Uncle Joseph was a warm and fun loving guy, so much like his father...my Grandfather Joe. I so much delighted in being with them both!

When Japan attacked Pearl Harbor and World War II began, my Uncle Joseph signed up to become a Chief Petty Officer in the Navy 'Sea Bees'. This special Naval unit was largely made up of construction specialists and engineers—building the airfields, bridges, housing and infrastructure needed once an amphibious force had secured a beachhead...or after a land invasion had taken enemy territory. But Uncle Joseph had a specialized assignment. His job? To build and manage the baseball fields and other recreational venues that were considered so critical to maintaining troop health and morale. Right after the airfield was built and the area secured, the sports field usually came next in priority. Throughout the War, Uncle Joseph was in the Pacific Theatre. Headquartered in Manila, he built ball fields in many recaptured Pacific islands.

My Uncle Joseph was a bit older than most of the Navy Sea Bees when he volunteered at age 35. But his son, my Cousin Bobby, was only 17 when he volunteered as a Navy seaman. While his Dad was in the Pacific, Bobby served in the European Theatre throughout the War. During the D-Day invasion, under heavy fire, he manned one of the landing crafts transporting ammunition, tanks and troops to Omaha Beach and Utah Beach. Thankfully, both Bobby and his Dad returned home without injury! After the War, Uncle Joseph separated from his wife Rose, but they remained close throughout their lifetimes. After the Navy, he worked for a number of companies before securing a position as Property Manager of a mixed-income complex called The Troy Towers. He worked there until his retirement and death.

My Cousin Bobby died in 2020 at age 95, outliving his dear wife (who was also named Rose) by just a few years. They had been happily married for 71 years and had 6 children, 19 grandchildren, 24 great grandchildren, and 7 great-great grandchildren by the time of his death.

❖   ❖   ❖   ❖

<u>My father...George Edward Warner</u>...was the oldest of many children born to Charles and Edith Warner. I say "many" because family lore says that...counting stillbirths and childhood deaths...there were more than a dozen. All I know for sure is that as a kid I had five loving aunts and over 14 first cousins on the Warner side. They all lived closely together in Watervliet.

My Grandfather Charles Warner had died before I was born, so I never knew him. But my Grandmother Edith told me that 'way back when' the Warner clan had come over from England. I'm not sure when they came over, or exactly from where. But Warner is a very old English name.

My Grandmother jokingly described her people as descendants of the Picts...the savage aboriginal people who painted themselves blue before attacking the Romans. This was her teasing way of saying they went way back, and came from the British Isles before the Europeans invaded. She was never more specific.

It may surprise you that I didn't even know my Grandmother Warner's maiden name. Not that it was a secret. It's just that things like that didn't seem particularly relevant in our family. Green Island, Watervliet, and nearby Cohoes were absolutely teeming with our relatives. As a kid, it seemed that everyone I met was introduced as a second cousin, or great uncle, or someone's brother-in-law once removed. So I grew up just assuming that everyone in our Town and area was somehow related! (They probably were!) Now I know that my Grandmother Warner's maiden name was McLoughlin...based on some old letters among my Mother's papers.

With such a large family, my Grandfather Warner needed several sources of income. I'm not sure what they all were, but they included running a tobacco store in Watervliet (with perhaps a poker table in the back room)...and a small fleet of rowboats to carry workers across the Hudson directly to their workplaces in Troy. (In winter, he'd set up a plank walkway across the ice.) The fare was 2¢ each way, the same price they charged pedestrians on the railroad bridge that was two miles north. His customers wouldn't save any money, but could cut a 4-mile hike off their commute each morning and evening. Meanwhile, he was a full time Lock Operator on the Erie Canal...a career my father later followed. In fact, many of the Warner men had links to the waterways. A great uncle captained a riverboat on the Hudson and another captained a steamer on the Great Lakes.

❖   ❖   ❖   ❖

Both my mother and father...Ann and George... were New York State employees...a godsend in surviving the Great Depression. He was Chief Operator of Lock #6 on the Erie Canal. She was a Fingerprint Expert in the NY Department of Correction. He worked in Waterford, NY and she in Albany. My Grandmother Warner lived with us for a few years after I was born, making it practical for my mother to go back to work pretty soon. Then once I started school, my Grandmother Warner went to live with her daughters in Watervliet...and my mother hired some very sweet local ladies who were looking for a little extra income. Once I was a little older, my maternal grandparents, Joe and Rita Teson, who lived right next door...were all that I needed. After Grandpa Joe died and I was away in college, my Grandmother Rita came to live with my parents.

Back when I was a kid, it was a pretty rare thing to have both parents working. Most Moms were at home all day to "keep the house" and "raise the children". But in my case, I'd be with my parents for only a few hours each workday evening. So we made the most of our weekends and annual two-week vacation. But even that time together was cut short during the war years. Due to manpower shortages and the critical role of the Erie Canal, my Dad had to consistently work a six-day week, and totally forgo his summer vacations. All this made the time we had together extra special.

It was typical back in those days for most fathers to head out to the local tavern after dinner every work night ...to "unwind" with their buddies. Not my Dad. He was home with us every evening. While he smoked, he just about never drank, except for a glass of wine at Holiday Dinners. My Mother would join him with a small glass of wine, but she never smoked.

Once a week or so, we'd visit my Dad's family in Watervliet... with the adults playing cards in the kitchen and we kids playing games in the living room or yard. On weekends, we'd often take a local drive...sometimes inviting my Aunt Irene to join us. In the summer, we'd often go for a swim in an area lake or creek. Fear of polio had most folks avoid the public swimming pools.

It was a happy life. My Mother was very sweet and gentle. My Father...kind and hard working. They never fought or argued. I never heard a swear word or witnessed any unkindness that either spoke. They were good and devout Catholics. I was blessed with truly wonderful, self-sacrificing parents!

I was never punished or even criticized. And looking back, that was probably because I didn't want to do anything that might jeopardize their approval and unconditional love. So I never broke any rule. Never talked back. Never rebelled at any age. Any urges that I might have had to do so, I kept bottled up and unexpressed. Then, as now, I believed that any hurtful words spoken can never be taken back. It may feel good to get them off your chest, but they'll remain forever as wounds in the hearts and minds of those you've attacked.

But there was certainly a downside to this kind of relationship. I can honestly say that I don't recall ever having had a serious discussion with either my Mother or my Father. I never shared a single worry or concern, or ever sought their advice. We didn't discuss or compare views on anything of substance. We loved each other, and that was enough. But even so, my parents undoubtedly had a major influence on my decisions in life—by example if not in words!

❖ ❖ ❖ ❖

What was it like living in Green Island in the late 1930s and early 1940s? If you've seen the Jean Shepherd movie "A Christmas Story", you'll have a pretty good idea of boyhood life back then. Working class neighborhoods, with small houses on small lots. Fairly large families, with everyone in the neighborhood seeming to know each other (most actually grew up in the area.) Lots of kids running around. Most houses had only one bathroom, one telephone (a party line), no washing machines for either clothes or for dishes. And only a few homes had an electric refrigerator (most had an ice box with deliveries by the iceman as needed). And only one-in-ten had showers (you took your tub bath weekly). Usually, there was just one fairly old car to the family, parked outside because few had garages. The coal furnaces were always temperamental and required shoveling in coal and taking out the ashes.

We had radios and record players, but no TV. As kids, most of us listened faithfully to a few of the after-school 15-minute radio serials (Dick Tracy, The Lone Ranger, Sky King, Little Orphan Annie, etc.). We saved cereal box tops to get decoder rings from advertisers. And like little Ralphie in "A Christmas Story", we always begged for a Roy Ryder BB Gun at Christmas. (I got one and never put my eye out!) We had simple bikes without adjustable gears, and made scooters from boards and old roller skates. We could roam freely as long as we were back home when the streetlights came on. And like Ralphie, we had an archenemy. Mine was a bully named Hunky Stebbins. He and his pack would raid our forts, knock over our games, and beat us to the ground whenever he caught us. One time my Dad told me to march right up to Hunky Stebbins and give him a big punch in the jaw, to teach him a lesson. I tried, but Hunky bloodied my nose while I was still working up courage.

I had a number of playmate friends in my pre-school years, and several more after I entered first grade at St. Joseph's School, which was about five blocks from our home. Everyone walked or rode their bike to school, there were no school buses back then, and most Dads needed the family car to get to and from work.

As kids, we boys usually wore knickers with high socks and leather boots that had a small clasped pouch to hold your jack-knife. The girls, of course, wore dresses.

❖   ❖   ❖   ❖

School Days...The four 'R's—
As Catholics, my parents sent me to Catholic School, where we were taught by the Sisters of Saint Joseph. We didn't have a kindergarten in Green Island, so I entered first grade directly at age five. There were 19 boys and girls in my class...the Class of 1949.

I really liked school. There was so much to learn and discover. I was anxious to take in as much as possible, so I always sat down front and tried not to daydream too often. The nuns were nice but insisted on discipline. We started each day with a prayer and The Pledge of Allegiance. An occasional ruler rap on the knuckles kept us from cutting up or passing notes around.

At Saint Joseph's we learned the four 'R's—Reading, Writing, Arithmetic...and Religion. That last 'R' was not allowed to be taught in Public Schools, even though Religion was once considered to be an essential part of every child's basic education. A study of Religion was once seen as very important, because 'personal morality' was deemed to be a critical element in any well-functioning and healthy society.

Public School kids can, of course, go to Sunday School...and some do. But most Catholics today are exposed to little or no theology, other than a 10-minute sermon when they attend Mass. So it's not surprising that so many Catholics have a somewhat incomplete or distorted view of their religion...or describe themselves somewhat proudly as "lapsed Catholics".

My eight years at Saint Joseph's were happy and productive. I learned a lot and liked all my classmates. But looking back, three negatives stand out—

1. I ended up a terrible speller. The nuns used the 'sight recognition' method of teaching words and reading. They'd hold up a card with a word and we'd shout it out, as quickly as possible. We never even heard of 'phonics', where you'd piece together a word by its syllables and sounds. We just blurted out the word that we saw on the card...most often mispronouncing it or even totally getting it wrong in an

attempt to be first and fastest. For example—"Hypotenuse" was shouted out as "Hippopotamus" to great laughter. The whole purpose of 'sight recognition' was to get us to read quickly. So the subtleties of correct pronunciation were never emphasized. And to this day, I'm never sure whether it's "particuler" or "particular"..."library" or "Libary"... "surprise" or "surprize"...Miniture" or "miniature". And once in a college paper, I spelled "incensed" as "incest" to the gleeful mockery of my Jesuit professor. Thank god, we now have Spell Checker!

2. I received a big dose of 'guilt'—People often kid or complain that in Catholic School the nuns teach you guilt. (At least on a par with Jewish Guilt.) It's true to a large extent. But a little guilt can be more of a blessing than a burden...because a little guilt can often help you make the right decisions. (Perhaps a better word than guilt is "a right conscience").

    It all starts, of course, with the Ten Commandments..."Don't do this."..."Don't do that." Eight of the ten forbid something. Only the Third (*Keep Holy the Lord's Day*) and the Fourth (*Honor thy Father and thy Mother*) are positive. Most of us really don't like rules and regulations. So we see the Ten Commandments as restrictions on our freedom and our free will. But consider another way to look at them. Consider instead that their real purpose is to help us lead a righteous and happy life...telling us how to avoid those very human pitfalls that will ultimately bring us unhappiness and harm. Viewed that way, they're something of an instruction manual on successful living. (Something akin to..."Don't run with scissors.")

So far so good. But the nuns at Saint Joseph's went a little too far. They were so effective in teaching guilt that as a kid I firmly believed that if I were to be run down by a truck after committing even a minor sin, I'd go directly to Hell...passing GO and Purgatory on the way to damnation. Even a quick Act of Contrition wouldn't save me!

Impure thoughts, foul language, disobedience...they could all result in the same outcome. Did that traumatize me? No, but in effect it "toilet trained me" to the straight and narrow. And it explains why my wife teasingly described me as "a borderline prude"...and why to this day...I don't like crude language, dirty movies, and blue comics. (But I do love shoot-em-up thrillers!)

3. <u>I got some really bad career advice</u>—Maybe it was just post-Depression thinking in Upstate New York, but the nuns underscored the negative aspects of untempered ambition. In referring to Mark 8:36—*"What does it profit a man to gain the whole world but lose his soul."*...they warned us to be careful about worldly ambition and trying to reach too far. I remember actually being told—"If your father is a carpenter or a mechanic, please don't aspire to achieve more in life. Don't let ambition and greed blind you...risking your immortal soul."

I've asked others if they had ever been told something similar from the nuns, or from anyone else for that matter, when growing up. They all said—"Absolutely not!" And in fact, as you'll see later, the Christian Brothers in my high school and the Jesuits in my college emphasized almost the exact opposite...that you had an absolute obligation to stretch your talents to the fullest to attain the greatest possible achievement in life. That was much better advice!

❖   ❖   ❖   ❖

Fun & Games—
I did all the usual kid stuff with my neighborhood pals. But since I had pretty bad asthma and allergies, I was a very poor athlete and got kind of chubby. (My folks bought my clothes in the 'Huskies' department.)

During summer weekdays when I was a little older, I took the city bus to the Troy Boy's Club, where the full day was loaded with activities. We'd usually take a long hike to the big swimming pool in Prospect Park, and later play board games and try our hand at various craft projects. Weekends were with the family. In summer, that often meant clambakes or outings to a nearby lake or swimming hole...or just sitting out on the front porch or in the back yard. (There was no AC, so cooling off outdoors was a must.)

A few times I went away to summer camp—'Camp Tekakwitha' on Lake Luzerne, near Lake George. (St. Catherine Tekakwitha was a Native American saint known as 'The Lily of the Mohawks.) And many summers we took a 2-week family vacation to Atlantic City. Back then it was still an elegant place with big oceanfront luxury hotels and hundreds of small rooming houses. During the War years, most of these rooming houses were packed with servicemen on leave, with foldup cots lining the hallways at night to accommodate as many as possible. The beaches were pristine, and everyone wore elegant clothes for their evening stroll or ride in a wicker rolling chair on the boardwalk. The shops sold luxury goods and some of the clerks wore tuxedos.

As a family, we also drove down to New York City at least twice a year...often with an aunt joining us. This was before the Thruway, so the trip took close to five hours. My father was a huge baseball fan, so he always took in a Brooklyn Dodgers Game if they were playing. I accompanied my mother and aunt to Macy's, Gimbels and other big department stores. They loved shopping, and I could spend time on my own in the stores' huge toy departments. Macy's even had a Magic Department, where a professional magician would give amazing demonstrations. I'd save up my allowance so that I could buy a few tricks and dazzle my pals when I got back home. On Times Square, there was another Magic Shop; and a place that sold the first full-head rubber Halloween masks that I had ever seen. My realistically scary Frankenstein mask made me the envy of all the kids in Green Island.

Halloween was a big deal for me. I made my own costumes to compete in the Troy Halloween Parade, where prizes were awarded. I turned this into a little business, making unique costumes for my pals. (A Mechanical Man, an Ice Cream Cone, a Shipwrecked Man on a Float, etc.)

As an only child and with both parents working, I had lots of alone time to devote to hobbies. Mine was making things— model airplanes and ships, of course. But also puppets, small

41

buildings and little dioramas. I also did a little oil painting. Later, I built some large things to decorate the front of our house for Green Island's annual 'Christmas Decorations Contest'.

In my earlier description of Green Island, I mentioned the Gilbert Car Works. Well, it was my good fortune that one of its premier artists...David Lithgow...lived just a block away and carpooled with my mother each day to his studio in Albany. (Born in England in the late 1800s, Mr. Lithgow was classically trained and was always immaculately dressed...with frock coat, cravat, wing collar, pince-nez glasses, and black derby hat.) Thanks to my mother, Mr. Lithgow invited me to his studio and introduced me to the fine arts. Many of the public buildings in the area displayed his large murals. His portraits of current and past governors lined the State House.

And he created the seven life-size dioramas of the 'Indian Tribes of New York State' that were housed in the 'NY State Education Department' building. As research to create them, he actually lived with each of the tribes for a week or more, as he made sketches and collected artifacts, garments, etc.

And if that weren't enough, another gifted individual lived in the neighborhood. Unfortunately I can't remember his name, but he showed us kids his workshop and the amazing models he built for display in the 1939 World's Fair and in the Natural History Museum in Albany. Using metals and other materials, be built miniature authentic working models of steam engines, riverboats, granaries, factories, saw mills, distilleries, textile mills, and much more. The detail and workmanship was incredible. It was far beyond our abilities, but inspirational in showing what could be done!

I was never a musician, although I did study piano for five years, with dismal results. My mother's bridge club friends all had daughters who were taking piano lessons. So my mother decided that I should study piano too. (At Saint Joseph's we didn't have music classes...or art classes, or health classes, or anything else other than the 4 'R's.) I never practiced for more than a few minutes a day, and no one ever taught me about chords or any of the basic musical concepts. All I learned was that when you saw certain spots printed on the sheet music, you hit certain keys. Why they went together, I didn't know. My fifth year piano recital ended my musical career. I somehow couldn't find the opening chord to my recital piece and made four or five random tries. The audience apparently recognized I was not playing an avant-garde atonal work, so a mix of laughter and gasps filled the room. As we left the hall, my father said—"That's enough! No more lessons!" While it was not a happy day for me, I was relieved!

I should add that there was no classical music radio station in the Troy/Albany area...and that I had never attended a classical music concert. We had no Church choir, and our organist played only some standard hymns. The only records we had at home were by Bing Crosby and his pop contemporaries. Suffice it to say...there was little inspiration to become the next Beethoven.

Four things I forgot to mention—
1. In 1940, before America entered the War, we drove all the way to Florida for a month-long winter vacation. This was before

the Interstate Highways, so it took us several days to get there. I was only 4 at the time, so my memory of events is a bit spotty. But I'm told the challenge on the road was finding places to eat that sold pasteurized milk. Raw unpasteurized milk back then could contain a number of life-threatening pathogens, and fear of contracting polio was real and widespread. Back in the 1940s, most all the restaurants and diners along the roadways were small locally owned places...and lodging was mainly in cabin courts, unless you went into city centers. Motels and Fast Food chains hadn't yet been invented!

2. During the summer, I'd often accompany my father to work at Lock 6 on the Erie Canal. It would be just he and I for the full day. He'd let me work the controls, opening and closing the canal gates and lowering or raising the lock water. Often, a tugboat captain would welcome me aboard to sail to the next lock, where I'd hitch a returning vessel to Lock 4. This was during and just after the War, so the canal boats were piled high with bauxite ore, or sulfur, or scrap metal...and the barges were full of high-octane aviation gasoline. Gas for cars was of course rationed. But occasionally, a barge captain would ask if my father had a bucket and rope. He'd lower the bucket into the barge hatch and fill it to the brim with five-gallons of gas for our old rumble seat clinker. Man, how that could travel! Gasoline, by the way, was rationed not because there was a shortage of gasoline or because it was needed for the War effort. It was rationed to reduce driving-related tire wear. Synthetic rubber hadn't been perfected yet, so tires were made from imported natural rubber... which came mainly from Japanese-controlled territories.

Lock 6 was fringed by woods, lakes and waterways...the perfect place to play and fish. We'd eat sandwiches we brought from home and drink cool natural spring water. My father brought a big thermos of coffee. It was fun! He was a self-taught electrician and showed me how to do basic wiring. And together we'd make boats and trucks out of pieces of scrap wood.

3. Most Friday evenings we'd have a family night out in Troy. All the stores were open and the streets crowded with shoppers. Weeknights my father did the cooking. (He got home from work just after 4:00pm...my mother not until after 6:00pm.) But Friday it was dinner out either at *Callahan's*... Troy's fanciest restaurant, with tuxedo-clad waiters and a 3-course "Blue Plate Special" for $1.00. Or we'd eat at the nearby YWCA cafeteria...where the Friday night special was Chicken à la King, with a green Jell-O salad embedded with carved carrots that looked like little gold fish.

After dinner and a little shopping, we'd buy a large container of Carmel Corn and drive home in time for our favorite radio quiz show—"Doctor IQ"...where the announcer would holler out—*"Doctor, I have a lady in the balcony!"* And her prize...if she answered the Doctor's question correctly? *"A box of twenty-four Mars candy bars!"*

4. When I was 12, my parents considered me old enough to take the Sunday train to New York City, with just one or two friends of the same age, for an exciting day in the big city. We'd arrive in Grand Central Station in late morning,

have a quick lunch at the Automat, and then go to Radio City Music Hall for the movie and amazing stage show. After that, we'd explore Times Square and have dinner at Toffenetti's. The 7:00pm train would carry us back to Troy, where our parents would pick us up for a fast drive home. We'd repeat our NYC outing once a year for the next few years, without incident or worry by our parents. NYC was that safe, and at 12 we were considered mature enough to keep out of trouble. We paid for our outings with saved up money from our snow shoveling.

❖　❖　❖　❖

There was lots more too. All the usual stuff kids do. Most of it fun!

❖　❖　❖　❖

To the modern reader, my childhood must sound like something from the Middle Ages or from a vintage movie. But I've described it here in great detail to help you understand the environment that shaped me.

❖　❖　❖　❖

REFLECTIONS
—on my childhood—

Many experts say that our experiences in childhood have a profound impact on our entire future life. (That's generally true; but over the years I've seen many exceptions...both positive and negative. And I've seen the pronouncements of many self-styled experts totally debunked.) But to establish a base point, I'll try to summarize the attitudes and beliefs I held at the end of my childhood years—

Views I held strongly at age 13—
- Always follow the rules and avoid confrontation.
- Don't say anything you'll later regret.
- Work hard and be very frugal.
- Find pleasure in making and creating things.
- Keep your eyes wide open to take in and absorb as much as possible.

And the negatives I carried with me?
- I was very shy and totally non-assertive with strangers.
- I was chubby and non-athletic.
- I had no idea what I wanted to achieve in life.

❖ ❖ ❖ ❖

As children, we don't live independent lives. We don't make truly independent decisions. We're shepherded by family and teachers...and shaped by the attitudes and circumstances of the age in which we live. But for how long do those childhood influences dominate?

Do we begin to shed them at age 'seven'...when we reach our so-called *"Age of Reason"*? Or do we shed them only once we reach our teenage years? Or do they actually dominate "forever"... as both Aristotle and St. Ignatius Loyola have said—*"Give me a child till he is seven years old and I will show you the man."*

Most modern psychologists agree that age 'seven' is indeed the critical transition point...the age where we start making our own independent decisions. But what makes age 'seven' so pivotal? The neuroscientists have an explanation—

"The most influential changes in the brain occur at age seven. Most notably, the frontal and temporal lobes grow enormously, more than at any other time in a person's life. Those lobes control cognitive functions and set the foundations for a person's capacity to learn, to get along with others, and to respond to life's daily stresses and challenges."

So at that point...age 'seven'...we apparently become mentally equipped to make our own decisions—asking ourselves new questions, expanding our sources of influence, and reaching out beyond family and teachers to embrace much greater independence. And all that is very healthy.

But for me...and I suspect for many others reaching age seven during the midst of World War II... our external influences remained pretty much unchanged up to and maybe even beyond age thirteen. So our childhood beliefs and attitudes held steady for much longer...exerting far greater influence on our future lives. We were the classic "seen but not heard children" even as we entered high school!

❖ ❖ ❖ ❖

Today we have a dominant and highly influential 'youth culture', which didn't exist at all when I was thirteen and just entering high school. Back then, we had absolutely no teen-oriented music, movies, clothing styles, magazines, etc. to influence us. And of course, there was no TV and no Internet. The record player was in the parlor, and your folks controlled what was played. Simply put—back then there were only two basic categories of people...children and adults. And in my time you were considered a 'child' until you became a 'young adult' at age eighteen and left home. Demographically speaking, there were just too few teenagers in my generation to make catering to us a potentially profitable market! Birth rates were low during the Great Depression and World War II. And we didn't have much discretionary money to spend.

It would take another five years until the post-WWII 'Baby Boom' generation would come of age...as the hundreds of thousands of kids born to returning GIs reached their teen years...creating a massive new market, with plenty of money to spend. Then, for the first time in history, "Teenagers" would become the marketing focus. And the "Youth Market" would come of age...with all that this implies!

So for me...as far as I can recall...the big changes in my attitudes and views never occurred at age 'seven'. They only began in my high school years at LaSalle Institute. That's where I made my first independent decisions. And that's the place where I met my first Mentor!

❖   ❖   ❖   ❖

High School

LaSalle Institute – Class of 1953—

Decisions! The first truly independent decision I ever made was where to attend high school. At the time, that decision didn't seems particularly consequential, but it proved to be life changing for a number of reasons. The most significant being that it brought me in daily contact with two remarkable teachers...one who became my first Mentor...the second who became a true role model.

Green Island had its own high school...Heatly High...and most of my childhood friends went there. In Troy there were two Catholic high schools...the co-ed Catholic Central High School and the all-boys LaSalle Institute. After comparing the three, I chose LaSalle.

Who knows where the other options might have led. But the chances are that after high school at either Heatly or Catholic Central, I would have studied engineering at RPI (Rensselaer Polytechnic Institute), lived at home during and for a time after college, and ultimately settled in the Tri-City area of Troy/Albany/Schenectady. None of that happened, and LaSalle was the reason.

As it turned out, I essentially left home and the area just one week after my high school graduation...coming back for never more than 2 or 3 weeks at a time. But more about that later!

❖ ❖ ❖ ❖

LaSalle was a 4-year, Catholic, all-boys military high school, with a student body of about 400. Students were called Cadets, wore West Point-style uniforms, became members of the U.S. Army Junior-Military Reserves, and earned various ranks in the Cadet Regiment based on the merits and demerits they amassed for performance in both academics and extra-curricular activities. From its beginnings until today, LaSalle was run by the Christian Brothers de LaSalle...the same order that runs Manhattan College in New York and more than 1,100 other educational centers in over 80 countries around the world. LaSalle's mantra, then and still today is "Truth/Duty/Honor".

To be accepted as a student Cadet, you had to take a comprehensive written test, followed by a fairly lengthy personal interview. In 1949, the annual tuition was $110, which included most of our uniforms. ($110 is about $1,000 today.)

LaSalle Institute had a long tradition in Troy. Founded in 1850, its mission back then was... "To educate and civilize rough and tumble boys"...which gives you some idea of Troy's rowdy population in the mid-19th Century. But by 1949, it had become a fairly prestigious college-preparatory day school, with an impressive record of student achievement and a long list of prominent alumni. It combined top-level academics with leadership training...all with an emphasis on personal character development in a God-focused environment. "Truth/Duty/Honor". That sounded perfect to me!

❖ ❖ ❖ ❖

Today, LaSalle is co-ed and has a middle school, with grades six through twelve. Enrollment is about 500 and tuition is now close to $15,000 per year. It boasts a spacious campus adjacent to Hudson Valley Community College, where LaSalle students can earn advance placement credits at no additional cost.

But back in 1949, we had far more modest facilities. LaSalle was headquartered in an 1878 four-story brick building in South Troy. Because of size constraints, only sophomores, juniors and seniors attended classes there. The rifle range and the lunchroom were in the basement. And a gym was in an adjacent, only slightly newer, one-story building.

The 100 or so freshmen attended classes in a reconditioned North Troy facility...Notre Dame Hall...where the athletic and drill fields were also located. Here we were divided into four homeroom classrooms of about 25 students each. We didn't move around between classes, the teachers came to us.

❖   ❖   ❖   ❖

So what made LaSalle so life-changing for me?
It began the very first day, when Brother Anselm entered our classroom and announced that he would be our homeroom teacher for the next four years, and that he would also be teaching us Latin and all our religion classes. He was a short, dour-looking man, with a haircut like Caesar and a build like Napoleon. During my four years at LaSalle, I rarely saw him smile...but from his actions, I could tell that he cared greatly for

us. In a sense, he was acting as a Drill Sergeant might, to bring out the best in us!

Then he said something that startled us all. As I recall it, he pronounced—

"If you do what I tell you, four years from now your parents will receive a gift of $10,000." That was a fortune, equivalent to over $112,000 today. He certainly riveted our attention!

After a long pause he added—*"That's because, if you do what I tell you, you'll receive a full scholarship to a top-level college...and you can tell your hard-working parents that the $10,000 they've been saving for your tuition will no longer be needed. That thanks to your efforts at LaSalle, they can now use that money for their retirement. It's your gift to them, with love, for all that they've done for you."*

Our unspoken stunned reaction? "Wow! That's incredible! But is that really possible?"

After another long pause, Brother Anselm answered the question we were all silently asking—

"You're no doubt wondering...how can I make this happen for you? It's because I've intensively studied the criteria that most major colleges use to award their scholarships. And I've developed an action plan that will let you move up to the top of their list of applicants. Implementing this plan will take your commitment and hard work, but the rewards are obviously enormous. And to help you every step of the way, I've received permission to be your

homeroom teacher and counselor for all of the next four years. But let me add this proviso—If your grades or commitment falter, you will not remain in this program or in my classroom. You'll be transferred into one of the other three classrooms...and be replaced by one of the other Cadets who demonstrate greater commitment. Now, you might ask...how did I get assigned to this classroom and not to one of the others? That decision was based on your test scores and the interviews when you applied to become a LaSalle student!"

And with that he began the roll call, asking each of us to stand in turn and briefly introduce ourselves, including the town where we lived, the number and ages of our siblings, and so forth.

❖　❖　❖　❖

Looking back on it all, I realize now that there was a brilliance in Brother Anselm's pronouncements. Then, as now, most students float half-heartedly through high school...bored by some subjects, not really seeing the need for others. The social aspects may be great...but for many, their high school studies are taken no more seriously than those in grade school.

In sharp contrast, Brother Anselm...on our very first day of classes...turned our entire high school experience into a true mission. He set out before us an enormously enticing and attainable reward...a huge gift for our parents...and a rich college experience for us...all within our reach only four years away.

In the fullest sense, Brother Anselm harnessed the motivational power that spells success in a winning sports team...and directly applied it to our high school academic studies. After his oration, high school for us no longer led to some generalized far-in-the-future reward. It led directly to a huge and attainable reward just four years away. A reward so enticing that there was simply no question that we should expend every effort to snag it. At age 13, he was offering us a win in what was effectively 'The Super Bowl of Life'. Vince Lombardi could have been no more motivationally persuasive!

And there was an important secondary effect. Before that day, most of us had never met before. But within just 15-minutes, the 25 of us had been effectively transformed into a unified Team on a common mission. The usual high school rivalries, cliques and pecking orders to separate 'winners' and 'losers' never happened. We would all be winners if we got with the program. And everyone approached it that way...helping a classmate if he was falling behind...sharing insights and ideas.

❖ ❖ ❖ ❖

Great! But what was the action plan we had signed on for? To understand it, I should point out that back then college scholarships were based solely on 'merit'—not financial need or demographics. And Brother Anselm's plan was designed to help us attain the highest possible 'merit scores' in each of four key areas—

1. <u>An Impressive Academic Record</u>—not only A+ performance in all the normal college prep courses, but also A+ performance in four advanced courses that most high school students normally can't fit in. For example—we could do all the course work for both Latin I and Latin II in our freshman year, simply by using our free study period and adding Saturday morning classes. And we'd continue that practice in our sophomore, junior and senior years with extra courses in math, languages and science. The NY State Regents Board would validate our performance, issuing us course credits if we passed their yearend exams.

2. <u>Impressive Test Scores</u>—Practice doesn't necessarily make perfect, but it can increase your speed and confidence. That's why Brother Anselm had us take IQ and SAT-type tests repeatedly during all four years. We'd chart our performance and identify the question-types where we were weakest, so that we could study-up as needed.

3. <u>An Impressive Range of Extra-Curricular Activities</u>—To show that we were well rounded, we were encouraged to add creative activities like the Glee Club and the Drama Club...and leadership activities like the Student Council and the Pep Club. Also, we were encouraged to become active in the language and science clubs, the school newspaper, etc. All these were above and beyond our performance in athletics and the Cadet Regiment. (An added benefit at LaSalle was that each extra-curricular activity earned you Merits that would ultimately determine your rank in the Cadet Regiment.)

4. <u>Acing The Scholarship Tests</u>—Back then, almost every college scheduled and supervised its own scholarship test, using one of the standardized tests developed and issued

by a national educational testing firm. In our senior year, Brother Anselm scheduled us for every scholarship test held in the Troy/Albany area. Some months we took four or five tests. With each test, our speed and confidence grew. And not surprisingly, on more than one occasion we found the exact same test that we had taken the week before. I guess you could call us "Test Sharks"!

So how did it all turn out? The 24 students remaining in Brother Anselm's class won 108 full college scholarships. (I won four. More on that later.)

❖　❖　❖　❖

Our education under Brother Anselm included far more than academics. He treated us like young adults from Day One. By today's standards, a number of his actions would raise eyebrows, if not arrests. But we loved them! Here are a few—

"Preventive Discipline"—
LaSalle was a military school. And in the military they'd always start you off with 'Boot Camp'...or in the case of the Service Academies 'Plebe Summer'. The idea was to turn "Mama's Boys into Men"...or in official lingo—"To re-socialize new recruits". Which the military defined as follows—"To submerge individuality and achieve discipline. And to create a bond of mutual loyalty among members of the corps."

At age 13, Brother Anselm 're-socialized us' using a milder form of Boot Camp. Each morning for the first two months, he'd call out a Town and if you lived there you'd have to stand up at attention. Then he'd pass down the aisles and give each of the designated Cadets a smart slap on the cheek. He called it "Preventive Discipline". No one was injured, and after the first few days everyone found it amusing. It became our "Today-you-are-a-Man" rite of passage and it got everyone wide-awake for our morning classes. (I was the only Cadet from Green Island and was therefore overlooked. My Town was never called, so I was never slapped. I never complained!)

<u>Girls, Girls, Girls</u>—
We were an all-boys school, so girls had to be imported for our occasional Friday night dances. As freshman, it was just a record hop in the gym. Brother Anselm knew most of us were pretty shy when it came to girls, so he created a Super Ploy to get us all enthusiastically up on the dance floor. He announced—
"Two months from now we'll be holding a Tea Dance and you'll all be there. Who knows what a Tea dance is?" Being hicks from upstate New York, none of us knew. So we just guessed—"A dance where they serve tea?" He said—*"Right! But we'll be holding it on a Sunday afternoon at 2:00 PM, not at night."*

Noting our total lack of enthusiasm, he laid out the plot—
"We'll send RSVP invitations to every young girl from every high school in the area...and those accepting will all be given a name tag with a small alpha-numeric code in the bottom corner. Your mission is to have a single dance with as many of your assigned girls as you can—rating them on personality, brains, family means, and good looks. You'll all be trained in asking the right questions to quickly come up with your ratings. After each dance,

you'll then go behind the curtained wall to enter your ratings into a numbered logbook. This will let us come up with a short list of the cutest, brightest, best-connected girls in the area. These are the ones we'll be inviting to all our future nighttime dances. The ratio of girls to boys at our Tea Dance will be over 3-to-1. That's why you'll have to limit your dances to just one per young lady. And remember, everyone deserves to be danced with. Some beauties are absolute duds. Some plain girls are true gems!"

The plan worked. The Tea Dance was a huge success. And none of us remained too shy to ask a girl to dance...or at a loss for words with the ladies!

Cocktails—

In our second year, the formal "Sophomore Soiree" was just weeks away. And Brother Anselm surprised us again with his lecture on 'Cocktails'. His opener—

"I'm not going to tell you not to drink, because I know you will anyway."

(At age 14 or 15, that was not only illegal, but the furthest thought from our minds.)

"But when you drink, don't be a boor. Don't guzzle beer. Sip a cocktail like a gentleman. And don't give your date Singapore Slings or some other one of those sugary drinks that will only cause her to upchuck in your Father's car. Order her a respectable cocktail."

He then proceeded to diagram our cocktail options on the blackboard.

Of course, none of us...I'd bet...actually drank cocktails at or after our "Sophomore Soiree"...or beer either. But that lesson

stayed with us for many years, through and beyond high school. *"If you're going to drink, don't be a boor. And don't order your date some sickening concoction."*
After all, at LaSalle we were trained to be Officers <u>and</u> Gentlemen!"

<u>The Right College</u>—
Attending for free was not the only goal. Selecting wisely to give us a leg-up on a future career was of equal importance. The question then was what career did we wish to pursue? Brother Anselm emphasized that we were not too young to learn about and consider our options now!

At Saint Joseph's in grade school, the nuns had warned us about reaching too high. At LaSalle, we were trained to reach as high as we could...and then reach even farther. And Brother Anselm took the lead in our training.

This is not to diminish in any way the importance of all my other Christian Brother and lay teachers and military instructors. All were uniformly excellent and influential. But Brother Anselm was in a class by himself. My first true Mentor!

❖   ❖   ❖   ❖

In my sophomore year, now at the South Troy campus, another Christian Brother played a major role in my development. Brother John taught me logic, geometry, civility, and cigar smoking.

While I had seen Brother John at many LaSalle functions, his course in 'Plane Geometry' was my first real experience with him as a teacher. My assumption going in was that he'd start the course with shape diagrams...the usual rectangles, triangles, circles, etc..... and the formulas to determine circumference, area, length, angles, etc. But it was a full two weeks before he showed us a single shape or presented a single formula. Rather, he introduced us to the world of logic and syllogisms. He showed us how to take two or more "knowns" to determine "an unknown". (For example—If all men are mortal. And if John is a man. Therefore, we can logically conclude that John is mortal.) Using this approach, he taught us the principles of "deductive reasoning".

Instead of asking us to memorize a series of geometric formulas that would long be forgotten, he showed us how to use logic to actually determine the formulas...and how to use logic to solve a wide range of problems. This provided us with the basis to understand not only geometry, but also the wider world of mathematics, science and even ethics. In hindsight, his was a remarkable approach. And it engaged us to relish every class he taught!

Brother John was tall and lanky, with a twinkle in his eye and a warmth that Brother Anselm rarely showed. More of a Jimmy Stewart to Brother Anselm's Humphrey Bogart. This made him extremely popular with both students and faculty, as well as with parents. He was a true role model. A real gentleman. Brilliant, yet self-effacing. Generous with his time and talent to all his students.

But what about cigars? We were rehearsing for our annual play...that year it was "Arsenic and Old Lace". I was playing the lead's evil brother, Jonathan. After seeing our rehearsal the night before, Brother John took me aside after class and suggested that I could make my character's brooding more menacing if I used a cigar as a hand prop. And he added—*"But you know, it takes some practice to convincingly smoke and handle a cigar. So, if you'd like, Brother Matthew and I would be happy to show you how to do it this afternoon, right after the lunch break."*

Brother John and Brother Matthew were so conscientious and generous with their time, that we three had cigar smoking practice sessions, not only that day, but every day right up until the show's opening. And lest I lose my cigar smoking skills, we got together for a refresher course at least weekly for the next two years. And that's how I became a cigar smoker at age 14. My Dad was a cigarette smoker, and my college roommates smoked pipes. I didn't care for either. A fine cigar can't be beat!

❖   ❖   ❖   ❖

LaSalle was a military school, so that of course played a big role in our education. Headed by a Captain in the U.S. Army Reserves, and staffed with Cadet Officers, the military program included classroom studies, marksmanship, and field drill maneuvers. As a Regiment, we marched in all the major parades in Troy, and our Drill Team and Honor Guard participated in many of the area's civic and patriotic events. Though music was not a subject taught at LaSalle, we did have a fine marching band that practiced as an extra-curricular activity.

While we had all the personal freedoms and high-jinks found in any ordinary high school, we adhered to a traditional military code of conduct. "Truth/Duty/Honor" was more than just a slogan. Minor infractions resulted in Demerits. Major infractions could lead to suspension or expulsion. But expulsions only rarely occurred.

As I mentioned, our uniforms were identical to those at West Point—and except for our shirts, they were provided to us by the school. Almost none of them were new. They were inventoried in a huge uniform storage room housed over the school's garages, across the back alley. Acquired from West Point and from various military high schools, they were hand-me-downs, passed along from class-to-class and student-to-student. (When I was a junior, I was appointed custodian of the uniform room. This earned me extra Merits and gave me the pick of uniforms. That explains why I had three 'non-regulation' greatcoats, with different reversible capes...a red, a blue and a gold, in addition to the standard gray. Except for the gray, I couldn't wear the others in parades and other official school functions, but I could wear the brighter colors at football games and for winter formal dances.)

❖　❖　❖　❖

At LaSalle, I made many new friends and a group of five of us stayed close palls well beyond high school. We lived in different towns...and fortunately one of us had a car. His folks also rented a big summer house on Saratoga Lake every year, where we'd often go swimming and water skiing. We also had a few pals from Catholic Central High School, along with several nice girls that we first met at our dances or when they were cast in our plays. Only one of my friends had a regular girl friend, although they never 'went steady'. But eventually, after college, they did get married. (In the late 1950s, the average age to marry was 23 for men and 20 for women.)

Movies, house parties, football and baseball games, dances, picnics, and late nights at the local diner—these were the usual places kids gathered in the early 1950s. It was all pretty much like the TV series "Happy Days" that first aired in the mid 1970s. (But no one I knew dressed like the 'Fonzie'...with his leather jacket and a T-Shirt with rolled-up-sleeves. If the local cops saw someone like that, they'd quickly 'escort him' out of town!) Of course there was no Rock-n-Roll yet, no coffeehouse folk singers, no hi-fi. But occasionally there'd be a big concert at the RPI Field House. There with my parents, I saw the 'Dean Martin & Jerry Lewis Show' and 'Johnny Ray'...whose record *The Little White Cloud That Cried"* was the first record I ever bought. It was a 78rpm that I played on a wind-up Victrola that was once owned by my Grandparents.

President Eisenhower was in the White House while I was in high school, and times were happy and good. After the trauma of a decade or more of depression and war, the country was rebuilding and enjoying a full return to normal life. The Korean War was now over and we were at peace. This period in the mid-1950s is often called "America's Golden Age for business and industry". And we were part of what they later called "The Silent Generation." All good! We were lucky!!

❖   ❖   ❖   ❖

<u>My First Jobs</u>—

Though I was pretty heavily loaded with studies and activities at LaSalle, as soon as I turned sixteen I applied for my 'working papers' and looked for a part-time job. I responded to a 'help wanted' listing in the *Troy Record* and was hired by "The Ideal Super Market" in Troy. I'd work Friday nights, Saturday afternoons and evenings, and full time during the summer. When I took the job, I didn't know that the turnover rate among their teenage employees was phenomenally high. Few lasted more than a week, no one for even a month. It's not that they were fired...they all quit because of the abusive treatment they received from the Store's owners.

"The Ideal Super Market"...which billed itself as *'Troy's largest independently-owned supermarket'*...was run by an Armenian family. The aged patriarch spoke little English (at least not in my presence) and was a butcher with a few missing fingers. The story went that in his old butcher shop many years before, the front door was always propped open during the winter to keep the meat fresh. His hands were so numb on one particularly cold day that he didn't realize he had chopped off his fingers with the cleaver, until he returned home that night and they started to bleed. He had two sons and a daughter who actually ran the business. Sonny was the butcher...dark and handsome and a bit crazed. Jimmy was older and the store manager. He had a crooked neck and was not blessed with good looks. He had a very sharp tongue and abrupt manner...but never with customers. Florence, the youngest handled accounting and supervised the checkouts.

The family actually owned two businesses—the Super Market, housed in a large one-story building…and a Wholesale Grocery Distributorship, housed in an adjacent but largely unoccupied three-story brick building. The fledgling Distributorship supplied canned goods and other non-perishables to many small Mom & Pop stores in the area. Both buildings had been part of a long-defunct old brewery

Like the other high school employees before me, I was mocked, insulted, verbally abused and ridiculed from the moment I joined the staff. I was given impossible tasks with no time to complete them. But being too stupid or timid to say "enough" and walk out the door to look for a better job, I voiced no complaint and tried to do everything they asked. Since this was my first job, I guess I thought that all bosses were like that. After all, it was their company and they were paying me to work there.

But a surprising thing happened. After my first month at 'The Ideal Super Market', their actions and attitudes toward me did a 'one-eighty'. They began to treat me almost like family. They said I was not like all those other kids who didn't want to work. They said I had proven myself, just the way they had to do when first learning the business! They then moved me to the meat department, where I became what they called a 'meat-counter man'. That move proved enormously beneficial!

I was still fairly shy when meeting new people, especially adults. But working behind the meat counter now put me in daily contact with scores of people. Gradually, I gained confidence in chatting up and even joking with customers of all ages. I found myself becoming something of a salesman...suggesting added purchases to take advantage of our "Specials".

Looking back, my 'education' at "The Ideal Super Market" was as valuable...if not more valuable...than my formal education. I went from being shy to being outgoing. I learned that a warm 'hello' and a genuine smile created a kind of bond, even with a total stranger. I learned that 'asking' and 'listening' were powerful keys to effective salesmanship. And most important of all—I discovered that when you return hostility with the exact opposite...kindness and understanding...that person's hostility usually melts away. Engaging in a retaliatory tit-for-tat may be human nature...but it usually ends in a lose-lose proposition!

All of these many lessons served me particularly well when I opened my own business many years later.

A few of the other things at the "Ideal" that prepared me to tackle work that was less than pleasant—Eviscerating hundreds of raw chickens, scraping and rewrapping dozens of moldy hams, and by far the nastiest of them all—an entire summer spent digging out a 3-story-tall stairwell in the old brewery that was encased top-to-bottom with a foot-thick layer of dried pigeon dung. (Some say that this last task was perfect training for my future work with clients in advertising.)

After my time at the "The Ideal Super Market", I had a summer job with the "Davy Tree Expert Company". They had a contract with the local phone company to spray the foliage under and above their overhead phone lines. I spent each day mixing and spraying the defoliants 2,4-D and 2,4,5-T from the back of a truck. Each night I'd return home fairly encrusted with the dried defoliants. It was only after the Vietnam War that I learned I was actually spraying 'Agent Orange'!

❖ ❖ ❖ ❖

My senior year at LaSalle was the best one yet. I wound up with the rank of Lieutenant Colonel...second-in-command of the Cadet Regiment. Among several perks was being invited to represent LaSalle at six formal high school dances in the area. Back then, that was the tradition among high schools. Since we wore our dress uniforms at formal dances, I didn't have to rent a tux. A corsage for my date ...not always the same girl...was my only expense!

As for Brother Anselm's promise of scholarships, I received four. Plus an offer of a possible appointment to West Point, which I declined. The scholarships included—
- Holy Cross as a Naval ROTC Midshipman
- The Coast Guard Academy
- Mount Saint Mary's College in Maryland
- Siena College in the Albany Area

Of them, I chose The Coast Guard Academy...which proved to be my first really poor decision!

❖ ❖ ❖ ❖

REFLECTIONS
—on my high school years—

The scientific and social science journals are filled with research papers and expert opinions on the physical, social, emotional and cognitive changes that occur during our teenage years. One key observation is that the part of the brain that governs our decision-making and impulse control...the *prefrontal cortex*... doesn't fully mature until we reach age 26. Before then, it's the *amygdala* that holds sway...with emotions and instinctive behavior largely in control of a teenager's decisions and actions. That may explain why so many teenagers make poor decisions or engage in questionable behavior.

There are exceptions, of course. And LaSalle did its very best to make us the exception. In academics, Brother Anselm laser-focused us on self-motivated personal achievement. Brother John and the rest of the faculty emphasized logic in problem solving and weighing options. The military program trained us in self-discipline and leadership. Our religious studies deepened our faith and expanded our understanding of natural law and morality.

All in all...my four years at LaSalle were truly transformative. I entered LaSalle as a shy 13-year old from a tiny upstate town...and left four years later as a confident, highly motivated, educated young man ready to leave home and enter the wider world. (Naïve, to be sure...because I really had no idea of the challenges that might lurk out there!)

But my next step was secure. The Coast Guard Academy was just two-weeks away.

<u>Views I held strongly at age 18</u>—
- You can achieve most anything in life...except perhaps fame...if you work hard enough and long enough.
- It's fun to actively engage with others.
- Ethical behavior ranks above all else.
- Never marry until age 35.
- New York City is <u>the</u> place to be!

<u>And the negatives I carried with me</u>?
- I was still totally non-athletic.
- My life experience to date was pretty parochial.
- I had zero experience with non-Catholics and all minorities.

❖　❖　❖　❖

College

Selecting my college—

I didn't particularly want a career in the military, which is why I decided not to pursue a possible West Point appointment. But the Coast Guard Academy and the Naval ROTC programs offered particular advantages. Unlike the Mount Saint Mary and Siena scholarships, both the Coast Guard and Navy scholarships included not only tuition, but also living expenses and a monthly stipend. In addition, both provided a full summer of adventurous training cruises and field maneuvers. (This far beat a summer job at a supermarket or spraying foliage.)

Of course, there was the question of active duty in the military after graduation and commissioning. Back in 1953, and continuing for the next twenty years, we still had the Universal Draft. At age 18, guys had to register with the Selective Service System and be issued a Draft Card. Then...unless you had a medical, college or other temporary deferment...you'd be inducted into the Army as a private, where you'd serve for a full 2-years. If you attended college under the Naval ROTC program, your contractual obligation after graduation and commissioning was 3-years. (Just 1-year more than the standard Draft <u>and</u> you'd be an officer, not a private.) The contractual obligation at the Coast Guard Academy was 4-years. (That's 2-years more than the standard Draft.) <u>But</u> their academic program seemed far more extensive...or so I thought!

So it all came down to an assessment of the future career possibilities that each of my short-list options offered—

- The Naval ROTC program let me choose my own major at a top-rated college. In my case, it would be Holy Cross and my major would be Chemistry. (I always loved science and knew there were great opportunities in the business side of the Chemical Industry.) I'd graduate and be commissioned at age 21...and after 3-years as a Naval Officer, I could enter private industry at age 24. Or...I could stay in the Navy if I so chose.

- At the Coast Guard Academy, I'd earn a BS in Marine Engineering and earn two-thirds of the credits necessary for an AB Pre-Law Degree...both valuable for a future civilian career. I'd be commissioned at age 21...and after 4-years as a Coast Guard Officer, I could enter private industry at age 25. Or stay in.

Weighing the pros and cons, I decided on the Coast Guard Academy. They gave me a specific date in late June to report in. This was about two weeks after my high school graduation. Upon arriving, I'd be sworn in and immediately go on active duty...starting with 'Swab Summer'...the Coast Guard's Boot Camp for new Cadets.

But fortuitously, I kept my options open with the Naval ROTC program at Holy Cross. They too had officially accepted me. And the next step would be my reporting in at Holy Cross after Labor Day...to be officially enrolled as a student and sworn in as a Midshipman. That was a full 2-months after my start date at the Coast Guard Academy. For some reason, I delayed telling them that I was not coming...and that I had selected another option instead. How amazingly important that decision <u>to not burn my bridges</u> with the NROTC and Holy Cross turned out to be!

❖   ❖   ❖   ❖

The United States Coast Guard Academy—
The Coast Guard Academy was located in New London, Connecticut, high above the banks of the Thames River...which flowed into Long Island Sound. Its piers berthed dozens of small craft and the 295-foot square-rigged training ship *Eagle*...a gleaming white Barque that had been seized from Hitler's Germany right after World War II. The *Eagle* sailed to distant ports each summer and throughout the year, manned by Academy Cadets. Other than the *U.S. Constitution*, she was America's only commissioned tall ship...and the only one to actually ply the seas.

The Coast Guard Academy differed from the other Service Academies in three ways—

1. It was far smaller...just 1,000 cadets vs. the 4,000 at both West Point and at Annapolis. (The Air Force Academy didn't yet exist.)
2. Unlike the other Service Academies...where the cadets were all political appointees...at the Coast Guard Academy you were selected based on a two-day battery of tests and personal interviews.
3. The Coast Guard's mission differed significantly from the Army's and Navy's. Theirs was—"To fight and win foreign wars and to deter aggression against U.S. interests." The Coast Guard's mission—"To ensure America's maritime safety, security and stewardship."

So all things considered, it was the Coast Guard Academy for me!

In June of 1953, just a few days after my LaSalle graduation, I packed my duffle and headed off to New London for my swearing-in ceremony as an active-duty member of the Coast Guard and life as a Swab!

Swab Summer went pretty much as anticipated—5:00AM bugle calls...a dash to the docks to lower-away our 8-man boats for a row over and back across the Thames...a run up the hill for a half-hour of calisthenics...a quick shower and change into uniforms...a "square meal" breakfast...then a full-day of classes and small boat handling lessons. After a sparse dinner, we moved into classrooms for two-hours of college-board tests. (The Academy was a beta-test location for newly developed prototype scholarship tests.) In between, we had snap inspections by upper classmen, with penalties like the "pile driver" and "air chair". For the "pile driver", you'd chin yourself in a doorway and extend your legs parallel to the deck. On the command "lower away", you'd abruptly let go and drop to the floor on your butt. Thus the name "pile driver". The "air chair" had you assume a sitting position in an imaginary chair, with your back pressed firmly against the bulkhead. You then extended both arms to the front and a rifle was laid across them. After several minutes, your joints locked up from the strain and you'd fall forward, still in that sitting position. You'd be carried to your bunk until your muscles relaxed and your legs and arms could be straightened out...usually within 10 to 15 minutes! Daily, there'd also be spot inspections of your room and uniform, with Demerits liberally applied.

Incidentally, a "square meal" was not a culinary term. It was a geometric term. At meals, a Swab had to sit rigidly on the front 2-inches of his chair...not permitted to move his head or eyes anywhere but from straight ahead...and only permitted to move his arms and hands in strict ninety-degree angles. He was allowed to eat only after all the upper classmen at the table had eaten their fill from the platters of food. Typically, there'd be only a few scraps left. While all of this may sound harsh, it was just "tough love" designed to shape us up. "Changing boys into men!" But not long after, the traditions of the "pile driver" and "air chair" were officially banned from all the Service Academies.

Yes, Swab Summer wasn't exactly fun. But none of that really had anything to do with my decision to resign from the Coast Guard Academy!

At a small group session one evening, led by a visiting Coast Guard Commander, I heard him brag that all the members of his Academy graduating class were still on active duty. I raised my hand and commented that this was very impressive, considering that we had only a four-year commitment to remain on active duty after being commissioned. His answer stunned me—*"That's true...but since the Coast Guard is undermanned, we haven't accepted the resignation of an Academy grad in over 20-years!"*

That's not what I thought I had signed up for! Plus, I was discovering that the Academy's BS in Marine Engineering was more about iceberg flow and climatology than ship design...hardly a career builder outside the Service. And that potential AB Pre-Law degree was almost exclusively about Maritime Law.

So the very next morning I went to a pay phone to call Holy Cross. I asked if they still had me listed as an incoming NROTC student. They said, "Yes" and that they were looking forward to my arrival in 10-days.

How fortuitous that I had delayed notifying the Navy and Holy Cross that I was not accepting my appointment in their Naval ROTC program. Keeping that option open proved to be one of the most important decisions I've ever made...because almost all the good things that followed in my lifetime flowed directly from that decision!

Later that same day, I officially tendered my resignation in the Coast Guard. Among the three interviewers hoping to dissuade me was a Coast Guard Chaplain. His admonition—*"Son...if you're a quitter here, you'll be a quitter all your life"*...left me speechless. I didn't want to tell him, or anyone else at the Academy, that I was switching to the Navy. My very reasonable concern was that they would try to sabotage my NROTC scholarship!

Once the separation papers were signed and safely in my hands, I packed my duffle and took a bus to the Greyhound Station. There, I called my parents and told them to expect me home late that night...and that I'd be heading off to Holy Cross the next week. Obviously, they were startled by all of this and wanted to know the whys and wherefores. That would come after I arrived home. I simply said that I had a better offer from the Navy.

The NROTC—In September 1953, my family drove me to Holy Cross in Worcester, MA. And we saw its beautiful campus for the first time. Naively, I asked an upper-classman if I was allowed to go off-campus with my parents...and if so, where I had to go to apply for a pass. He looked at me like I had just been released from a monastery or prison. The next surprise was in the Dining Hall. I had expected that we'd eat in total silence while a Jesuit read Scripture to us aloud from a pulpit or balcony. But not so! Instead, the Hall was alive with noise, laughter and horseplay. So this was a civilian college! And I loved it!

Even better, my future BS degree in Chemistry would give me many more career options. And there was just a three-year commitment as a Naval Officer.

At my official Navy Midshipman swearing-in ceremony, they asked—*"Are you on active-duty with any other branch of the armed forces?"* Honestly and emphatically, I could say "No!"

If you're keeping count, I had now officially served in three branches of the military—The Army (the JROTC at LaSalle), the Coast Guard, and now the Navy.

❖　❖　❖　❖

The College of the Holy Cross—
I really didn't know much about Holy Cross before receiving a notice from the Navy Department telling me that I had been awarded a Naval ROTC scholarship...and that I was to be assigned to their Holy Cross unit. There were 131 colleges in the

NROTC program, and as part of the original scholarship test, applicants were asked to select up to ten as their preferred colleges. Along with Harvard, Yale, Princeton, Notre Dame and five others, I had checked off Holy Cross. All I knew of the place then was that it was a highly-regarded Catholic liberal arts college located somewhere in Massachusetts...with great sports teams. (Back then, they had won the Orange Bowl, the College World Series, and both the NCAA and NIT Basketball Tournaments.)

After receiving the initial letter from the Navy, I obviously needed to know more about Holy Cross. So I called their Admissions Office and asked them to send me a Student Handbook and other background information. What I learned convinced me that Holy Cross should really have been my first choice among those ten colleges. It seemed a perfect fit for me! But still, I picked the Coast Guard Academy. Now, dumb luck, and perhaps something more, had given me this unplanned opportunity to attend Holy Cross...a move that led directly to my second Mentor...whom I would meet early in my Senior year.

❖　❖　❖　❖

Holy Cross had a long tradition...and in so many ways was unlike other colleges.

Founded in 1843, it was the first Catholic College in New England. Boston Bishop Joseph Fenwick had hoped to locate it right in central Boston, but the City's Protestant Civic Leaders blocked his efforts. So he chose Worcester, 44-miles away, but still in his Boston Diocese. To run the College he chose the

Jesuits...because he had long admired their unique approach to education.

The Jesuit system of education was called the *"Ratio Studeorum"* or Plan of Studies. Based on the Order's 450-year-old tradition, it emphasized... *"A unity of education to develop a student's knowledge and character."* Instead of what we today call... Freshman, Sophomores, Juniors and Seniors...Jesuit students were called Poets, Rhetoricians, Logicians and Theologians. And although these names are long gone, the curriculum still reflected those levels of study...or at least it did in 1953.

As I reviewed the 1953 Student Handbook, I saw that depending on your Major, every course was pre-assigned. There were few if any electives. As the Handbook explained—*"Your course of study is determined by experienced educators, not left to inexperienced students."*

Even as a Chemistry Major, I'd be receiving a classical liberal arts education that included—the humanities, rhetoric, mathematics, natural and social science, logic, philosophy, ethics and theology. All that in addition to the full range of science courses and related lab work...plus eight pre-assigned NROTC military courses. (To fit in the NROTC courses, Foreign Language studies were eliminated.)

Upon Graduation, I'd receive a BS in Chemistry & Philosophy and be commissioned as an Ensign in the U.S. Navy. In all, I'd be taking ten courses in Philosophy...all concentrated in my Junior and Senior years. These included—Epistemology, General

Metaphysics, Cosmology, Natural Theology, Fundamental Psychology, Advanced Empirical and Rational Psychology, General Ethics, and Special Ethics. Clearly, I'd be studying classic 'Scholastic Philosophy', based on the writings of Aristotle and St. Thomas Aquinas. (No modern philosophers here!)

Consistent with the *Ratio Studeorum*, every student would study Rhetoric during their Sophomore year to develop skills in argumentation, persuasion, public speaking, and debating. And every student would have to pass Oral Exams in front of a senior faculty panel in order to graduate.

If all this sounds pretty demanding, it was. But I figured it would give me a broad and solid educational base for whatever future career I might eventually pursue. Just learning Chemistry was not enough! Skills in logical thinking, discerning, speaking, persuading...along with unequivocally clear ethical standards and moral values...these I viewed as truly essential components upon which to build one's future life and career.

❖ ❖ ❖ ❖

After dropping me off and our taking a brief tour of the campus and downtown Worcester, my parents returned home and I went to unpack in my 4-person dorm room. It was on the third floor of one of the school's oldest buildings—O'Kane Hall. There were two metal bunk beds, four Army surplus plywood lockers, and four small beat-up desks with wooden chairs. Pretty basic...but the two very large windows gave us a commanding view of the campus drive and gardens below. Yes, the room was boarding school old, but it was spotless...especially the floor, which was covered in highly polished linoleum. The equally clean communal toilets and showers were located at the far ends of the hall. O'Kane would be my home for the next academic year!

I met my three roommates, all great guys! And as it turned out... and as you'll see later...the very best of them, Bill Sullivan, not only remained my Holy Cross roommate for the next three years...but we became related by marriage when he later wed my wife Anne's identical twin sister Barbara.

As now officially 'college men', all three of my roommates decided they had to buy pipes to complete their 'Joe College' image. So I joined them as we trekked down hill to the nearest off-campus drug store. I too bought a pipe and tobacco, though I had an ample supply of my first love...cigars.

Classes began two days later, and my first assignment was an orientation session in the Chemistry Department. There were only nine of us Freshman who were Chemistry Majors, but the Department's labs and lecture halls were quite large. That's because hundreds of Holy Cross students were in the Pre-Med program, and Chemistry as well as Biology were required courses.

Next stop was the Naval ROTC Department, headed by a Navy Captain and a Marine Colonel. In all, there were about 170 NROTC Cadets at Holy Cross, including the 42 new ones in our Class.

Except for Naval Science and Physical Chemistry, all of my courses would be taught by Jesuits. The Jesuit approach to teaching was 'tutorial' rather than 'professorial'... meaning a dialog with each student, rather than uninterrupted lecturing. Also, many of the younger Jesuits would live right in the dorms, acting as our corridor prefects. At the time, Holy Cross had 328 resident Jesuits. (Today Holy Cross-has twice as many students, but very few Jesuits still on the faculty. And as you'd expect, the curriculum and living conditions are now dramatically different.)

❖　❖　❖　❖

As I said, Holy Cross was in so many ways unlike other colleges back then.

It was fairly small...with only 3,100 students. It was all male. And there were no fraternities...so collegiality reigned campus-wide. There was no hazing or pecking order. Good fellowship and good cheer seemed the order of the day. Certainly there were cliques, but no animosity between them was apparent to me. We were all considered brothers in the same big family. Within a month, I had made a growing number of new friends... from New York, Boston, from all across New England and elsewhere around the Country. Some were fellow Chemistry Majors or in the NROTC, but most were English Majors or studying the Classics. We were learning so many new things from each other...that it significantly added to and expanded upon what we were learning in the classroom.

I should probably point out the central role of *Kimball Hall*. It was the massive and beautiful Dining Hall where we gathered together each day for our meals...eating family-style at tables set for twelve and served by student waiters. With its high coffered-ceiling, clerestory windows, painting-hung walls, and inlaid marble floors, it made even institutional food seem a bit special.

Three times a day, we'd all gather in the Quadrangle until *Kimball's* doors were opened at the precisely scheduled hours. As in our classrooms, jackets and ties were required. They say that gathering together as a family at mealtime is an important key to healthy family life. Thanks to *Kimball Hall*, we had that and more...joking, comparing notes, expressing concerns, asking for advise...we'd come together to eat and chat three times a day. And before each meal, we'd all rise as someone led us all in saying Grace!

I found all of this both stimulating and fun! But even in 1953, much about student life at Holy Cross was draconian compared to other colleges. And by today's standards it would seem absolutely Dickensian. For example... as Freshmen, we had 'lights out' at precisely 10:30PM. And our corridor prefect would visit each dorm room at both 7:00PM and 9:00PM to make certain we were in there studying. (One could get permission to study in the Library instead of your room, but that required a special Approval Pass.)

In addition, our attendance at 7:00AM Morning Mass each weekday was mandatory...and strictly monitored. If you missed three Masses in a two-week period, you were put "On Report". There were numerous other ways to be put "On Report"—cutting classes, not being in your room studying during room checks, sneaking back onto the campus if you were 'checked-out' for the weekend.

What was the penalty for being "On Report"? It was punching a time clock in the Dean-of-Men's Office, every hour on-the-hour from 7:00PM to 10:00PM on Friday night...and <u>all day</u> from 10:00AM until 10:00PM on both Saturday and Sunday. And because the Dean-of-Men's Office was located far downhill beneath the Dining Hall, it took over 10-minutes to get there from most dorms...and even longer to return to your room. As such, most students "On Report" just stayed near the Dining Hall...studying, reading, conversing, or playing catch. (I had one classmate who was "On Report" most every weekend for all four years.)

The drinking age in Massachusetts was 21, not 18 like in New York State. While most younger students had fake IDs to buy beer at local bars or Package Stores, alcoholic beverages were strictly forbidden on campus. If caught with beers or booze in your dorm room, you could be suspended. Repeat occurrences would result in expulsion. But even so, there were secret stashes of whiskey in many dorm rooms...but no beer, because we had no way to keep it both hidden and cold.

Even with all those restrictions, I found freshman life at Holy Cross terrific. Big football and basketball weekends... numerous stag dances, with hundreds of girls arriving from area colleges...frequent concerts and lectures...and most of all, just hanging out with friends. Later in the year, there'd be...Parents

Weekend, Homecoming Weekend, and the traditional exodus to New York City for St. Patrick's Day Weekend.

Time flew by! All was well! That is...until my grades were posted.

It was the day before our Christmas break...about mid-way through my first semester. At the top of the second floor landing in O'Kane Hall, a large group of students was clustered around a 40 x 40-inch glass framed poster affectionately called "The Christmas Tree". On it was a list of all of us freshman, with our grades posted for each course. If you had a failing grade, a red dot was affixed to that entry...a little red 'ornament' that was as welcome as a lump of coal! When I searched for my name, I was shocked to find three red dots. In high school, I routinely had high 90s or 100 in most all my subjects. But on "The Tree" I had a 33, 36, and 41 in three of my most important courses. Gulp!! And best yet, a letter to my parents would be sent to arrive just before Christmas, telling them of my failing grades. It was all designed to put maximum pressure on us to buckle down and reverse things in the remaining weeks of the semester. And it certainly worked. Since your pre-Christmas grade represented only one-third of your final grade for the semester, there was still time to recover! And I had to...because if I flunked out, I'd loose my NROTC scholarship and be immediately drafted into the Army as a private. (That was in the small print of the documents I had signed.)

But it all ended well. I didn't flunk out, although I was more of a B+ student in most of my courses. This sure wasn't high school anymore! At Holy Cross, I actually had to study!

The rest of my Freshman year went well, with lots of memorable things inside and outside of class, which I won't take the time and space to report here. But the final weeks had me focusing on getting ready for the NROTC summer cruise that I would be starting soon.

❖　❖　❖　❖

Norfolk, Virginia—

My 8-week Navy Training Cruise would embark from Norfolk, Virginia...and we'd be part of a large fleet with the famed battle-ship *USS Missouri* as flagship. My Holy Cross roommate, Bill Sullivan, was fortunate enough to be assigned to the *Missouri*, with its 2,700 crew members...while I was assigned to a small radar-picket-class destroyer, the *USS William M. Wood*, with a crew of less than 300. About one-third of the crews on most of the participating ships would be Midshipmen...replacing the enlisted crewmembers who were on leave. About half of the Midshipmen were from the U.S. Naval Academy in Annapolis and half were from various NROTC Colleges.

Specific shipboard assignments differed by seniority...rang-ing from Command Officer duties for those on their third year cruise...to Junior Officer duties for those on their second year cruise...to duties usually performed by the enlisted seamen, for greenhorns like me.

The first leg of our cruise involved 19-days of maneuvers in the North Atlantic and North Sea...with 7 of them under hur-ricane conditions. It all started out tranquilly enough, then the

Seas turned vicious. Our ship was tossed about like a toy boat... rolling side-to-side, while also plunging beneath-and-over 50-foot waves. We routinely took 47-degree rolls and all except the topmost deck were fully awash. All the lower hatches were firmly secured. Venture forth and you'd be washed away. The pounding of the waves was incessant, like some giant who was pounding to get in. And the constant creaking of the ship made you hope that the welders had done their job right.

About 80 of us were berthed in a narrow bow compartment... with fold-down, pipe-framed canvas racks stacked three high. Because the compartment's ventilating system was on the fritz, the temperature was close to 105-degrees and the stench of sea-sickness-induced vomit was pervasive. Add to that the constant fierce up-and-down, side-to-side rolling, and it was all pretty terrible. (After the cruise, Bill Sullivan told me that at its very worst, the *Missouri* was taking 3-degree rolls. Size does matter!)

I've been asked—*"Weren't you afraid your ship would sink?"* I could honestly answer—*"At the time, I wished it would."*

But then after the storm, calm seas returned. We had earned our sea legs. And we were now real Navy Sailors!

Life aboard the *William M. Wood* was demanding but congenial. However, duty hours kept you pretty exhausted...with never more than 4-hours of continuous rack time...even less when your assigned *'work station'* time overlapped your assigned *'watch duty'* time. Or when frequent calls to "General Quarters" had you rush to your assigned post. My *'watch duty'* assignments rotated weekly...radar, sonar, gunnery, engine room, navigation, weapons control, lookout, etc. My *'work stations'* included refueling, KP, and for the most part—polishing brass, chipping paint, and then repainting the same steel bulkhead again and again.

The food was hearty and plentiful. But during the hurricane period, it was mainly saltines plus oranges to suck on. A huge metal 'bug juice' pitcher hung from a rope, where it swung like a pendulum with the ship's motion. But for thirst, most of us just used one of the water fountains located throughout the ship... always downing a few salt pills from the nearby container, as required to help prevent dehydration. Incidentally, I also learned what they meant by a 'Navy Shower". Although the ship had a desalination plant, potable water was precious and not to be wasted. So your shower consisted of 3-phases—a 10-second burst of water to wet you down...then a minute or so to soap-up and scrub-down without water...then another 10-second burst of water to rinse away the soap and grime. Until all this became second nature to us, an upper classman with a stopwatch monitored our efforts.

After 19-days at sea, we entered our first port...Cadiz, Spain. And our 5-days in Cadiz added about five years to my life experiences. Throughout our cruise, many of the "white hat" seamen kept talking about the beautiful Spanish women and bragging about how many they would ravage. I took all that as bravado. But it proved to be far from mere bravado!

As we approached the docks, I saw over a hundred young girls in white dresses accompanied by their fathers. Naively, I thought..."*How nice. The local dignitaries and their daughters are here to welcome us.*" When we tied up and the gangplank went down, the on-shore scene changed abruptly. The girls climbed up onto boxes and their 'father/managers' started hawking their wares. It seemed, that as word spread across southern Spain that the U.S. Navy would soon be arriving, almost every prostitute in the region rushed to Cadiz. The youngest and prettiest were lined up on the docks, like living mannequin displays in a shop window to entice buyers!

On our first day and night in Cadiz, I had Quarterdeck Duty and had to stay aboard. We were tied up dockside, with four other destroyers tied up directly abreast. That meant that as many as 1,500 seaman and officers had to pass across our Quarterdeck to go ashore and then later return to their ships.

Along with three other Midshipmen, two sailors, and a 'Sergeant-at-Arms' Petty Officer, we would be checking everyone's documents and liberty passes to assure that ship security was maintained...and that no unauthorized personnel were permitted aboard. We had five heavily armed multimillion-dollar Naval vessels to protect!

Everything went smoothly as the men went ashore. But as nighttime fell, the horror show began! To say that the large majority of seamen, Officers and Midshipmen returned drunk and totally disheveled would be an understatement. It was sheer pandemonium! Some had to be carried up the gangplank. Five fell into the harbor. And twice we had to run off the ship to break up knife fights down on the pier. On the Quarterdeck, one totally drunk sailor took a swing at the Sergeant-at-Arms... who pulling back to avoid being struck, rammed his head into a steel stanchion, spewing bright red blood down his face and across his white uniform. Hearing all the yelling and cursing, a Ship's Officer (who seemed a bit tipsy himself) suddenly appeared on the Quarterdeck...dressed only in his skivvies and ominously waving a big 45-caliber pistol. We all froze as he verbally threatened to—*"blow that shithead of a sailor away!"* Another Officer appeared, took over, and ordered us to handcuff the offending sailor and transport him to the brig in our nearby Cruiser. I never heard for sure what happened to that sailor, but I was told he was most likely Court-Marshaled and sentenced to several years of hard labor in a Navy Prison. As they were getting ready to take the sailor away, I was ordered to remain on deck and mop up all the blood. Which I of course did.

Meanwhile, we got word that two rowboats had silently tied up at our stern and several locals were attempting to climb aboard. Searchlights and a display of our big handguns convinced them to quickly row away. Then we got word that another far bigger boat was circling near our furthest out destroyer...this one with several aging hookers aboard. They were calling out to invite some of our sailors to climb down and join them for "a little nightcap!" Quite a night!

The next day I had liberty, but had to be back onboard for another night of Quarterdeck duty. As I was logging out to go ashore, a Midshipman from Yale suggested that we share a horse cart and go to the beach for the day. When I asked the cost, he told me that we could hire a horse cart with driver for only 2-pesetas a day. (That was only 5-cents in American money!) Being a big spender, I agreed. The beach was great and our lunch at a shorefront café excellent. It cost just 1-peseta for the two of us, including wine and a generous tip. As we sat down for lunch, my new friend from Yale asked if I could speak Spanish. When I said "No"...he declared, with a condescending smirk, that then he'd better do the ordering for us. While still perusing the menu, he asked our waiter to bring us some *Agua Hirviendo*. The waiter looked very surprised, but then shrugged as he headed off to the kitchen. My friend explained to me that is was important to drink only 'boiled water' in Spain, because the local tap water wasn't safe. OK...I already knew that. But I had to conceal my delight when our waiter finally returned carrying a big steaming pot of 'boiling water'. (Later, I looked it up and found that the right word for 'boiled' is *Hervida* not *Hirviendo*, which means 'boiling'. And that he really should have ordered *Agua Embotellada*... which is bottled water. So much for that flaunted Yale education!)

My second night on the Quarterdeck was much like the first. But this time, even the returning Officers grabbed handfuls of the penicillin tablets from the box next to the sign-in podium. (We had been told that a highly contagious venereal disease was rampant in southern Spain and that penicillin was recommended to minimize infections.) As it turned out, about half the Midshipmen wound up getting VD and were relieved of work assignments until their rashes cleared up. They gloated over this as the rest of us drew double duty, while they just lounged about. But their attitude quickly changed when it was announced that anyone not symptom-free by the time we returned to Norfolk would be detained in the Base Infirmary and their parents and schools notified as to the reason.

During my final days in Cadiz, a small group of us were assigned to represent the U.S. Navy at a reception being held in our honor at the local Yacht Club. While there, we met a nice group of bubbly teenagers anxious to try out their English and learn more about America. Each of the girls was hovered over by a personal chaperone, introduced to us as their aunt or grandmother. The boys were cousins or brothers of the girls. When we asked if they'd like to dance, the girls explained that until engaged or married they were not allowed to join the adults on the dance floor.

As we chatted and answered their many questions about life in America, they offered to give us a personal tour of Cadiz the next day. Appreciatively, we took them up on their very kind offer...which would, of course, include their ever-watchful chaperones.

The next morning, three beautiful open-air horse coaches picked us up at the ship...to the surprise and envy of our gawking shipmates. The tour was exceptional, as we visited various parts of the City, explored the Cathedral and other major sites, and learned about the importance and rich history of Cadiz...a day peppered with laughter and good cheer. Our tour ended late in the afternoon with a marvelous buffet at the palatial home of one of the young ladies. Clearly, these were the kids of the Cadiz "Rich and Famous".

Cadiz! What a city of truly remarkable contrasts! Hundreds of beckoning prostitutes calling from upstairs windows along most dark side streets...and highly-refined young ladies with chaperones, who viewed even dancing before marriage to be immoral!

❖   ❖   ❖   ❖

After another almost three weeks at sea, we visited our next port, Rotterdam in the Netherlands. Spotlessly clean and fully rebuilt since its almost total destruction by Nazi bombers during World War II, Rotterdam was and still is one of Europe's major port cities. For reasons that required no explanation after the debauchery of Cadiz, the Navy made Rotterdam's 'Old Town' strictly off-limits for all Navy personnel... with severe penalties for violators. Holland is, of course, famous for its beers, but that was not the initial beverage of choice for we mariners. After more than a month from our last sip of fresh milk, the first stop for most of us was a local food store where we could buy a liter or two of icy cold milk. Then sitting down right outside on the curb, we savored each creamy mouthful. After that, we were ready to hit one of the nearby vending machines that stood on most every corner...dispensing their rich dark chocolate bars. What a treat!

Rotterdam was certainly very interesting to tour, but most of us took advantage of our three-day shore leave to take the train to Paris. There I visited all the famous sites that I could squeeze in, and snapped photo after photo with my new camera. Three of us shared a room in a small hotel...splurging our money on orchestra seats at the *Follies Bergere*, followed by a lavish dinner at a quaint garden cafe built around an ancient windmill. It wasn't the *Moulin Rouge,* but it did have a windmill...this one white!

Back in Rotterdam, I was assigned to attend an afternoon reception at the *Submariner's Club*...perhaps because someone thought I had done an OK job at the Yacht Club in Cadiz. I was running late and found my map and directions a bit confusing, so I asked a local Police Officer how to get there. Though he spoke perfect English, he didn't understand when I kept saying—*"The Submariner's Club."* Finally, in desperation and using both hands to demonstrate, I said—*"You know...a boat that can travel under the sea."* He then lit up and said—*"Aah... Der Onderzeeër Boat Club...that's what you want!"* I got there in time and it was great.

Our final port was the *Guantanamo Bay Navy Base* in Cuba. This was long before Castro and the revolution, but even back then we were all restricted to the Base. We were in Gitmo for gunnery practice only...and each day we'd sail out to fire our big guns at a succession of moored floating targets. Our proficiency was closely monitored and scored. And there was a great competitive spirit among the participating vessels. At sunset, we'd then return to shore and after chow visit the base canteen or catch a movie.

An interesting sidenote—One of my Holy Cross classmates happened to wander into a base warehouse, where a lively craps game was underway. When he showed he had a roll of cash, the dozen or so participating seamen invited him to join in. Five hours later, he had won over $3,000 (the equivalent of over $32,000 today.) Warned that he could be mugged, robbed, or even killed before returning to the States, a few of the sailors escorted him to the Base Procurement Office where he turned his $3,000 into 300 Navy surplus typewriters...to be shipped back to Worcester, Mass. There his father opened a small store, selling off the typewriters at a huge profit. Free enterprise at its best!

Steaming back to Norfolk, our 8-week training cruise was coming to an end. I wasn't yet exactly an "Old Salt", but I was no longer a "Greenhorn". I had experienced the vastness and awesome power of an angry Atlantic Ocean and North Sea. And learned an enormous amount about life and operations aboard a Navy Warship. I had visited Spain, the Netherlands, Paris and Cuba for the first time. I'd seen amazing sites, met many new people both on and off our Ship, been exposed to new cultures and attitudes, and witnessed vast extremes of behavior...from the grossly immoral...to the super prim and proper. All this, in just 8-weeks!

❖ ❖ ❖ ❖

Sophomore Year—
A few things had changed as we entered our second year. The Sophomore dorms were far nicer...and it was now two-to-the-room instead of four. Dorm rooms were awarded by a random lottery...when your name was called, you got your pick of what was left. Being called early, Bill Sullivan and I got a great location.

Also, the rules were loosening a bit. Just once a night room checks, and 'lights out' at 11:00 rather than 10:30. (Over the next two years, more and more restrictions would be dropped. But compulsory daily Mass and being put "On Report" were still going strong.) There were also extra options to keep we growing boys well fed. The cafeteria beneath Kimball Hall had more choices; and more vending machines had been installed throughout the campus. Plus every weeknight an upperclassman or two would swing through the dorms with a sack full of foot-long 'Grinders'. (That's what they called 'Heros' and 'Subs' in Worcester. Incidentally, they called their milkshakes 'Frappes'.) And we were hearing a new kind of music. One of our classmates had a "crystal radio set" that could pick up New York City...where a DJ named Alan Freed was playing something new called *Rock-n-Roll*.

It was 1954 and many changes were in the making nationwide. Senator Joe McCarthy had everyone on edge with his TV hearings, claiming the Federal Government and U.S. Military were rife with Communists. The Supreme Court had just issued its "Brown vs. the Board of Education" decision, declaring that school segregation was illegal. At a place called Bikini Atoll, the U.S. set off something called a 'Hydrogen Bomb'. And the words..."*Under God*"...were added to the Pledge of Allegiance. Also a young senator from Massachusetts...a Catholic named Jack Kennedy...was making moves to run for the Presidency.

Like young people coming of age in every generation, we certainly craved some grand cause to get behind...something big and important to throw our energies into...in order to achieve

meaningful change. But after going through the list of possibilities one-by-one, we rejected them all as being 'un-doable'.
Our bottom line conclusion—"We just didn't have the clout to
effectively "Fight City Hall". (I'd argue that the Vietnam protests in the 1970s largely resulted from that same underlying
'primal youthful urge' that we had back in the 1950s. But that
they succeeded then, only because the 'Baby Boom' generation
had grown large enough that they could at last "Fight City Hall".
Demographics made all the difference! At least that's my take
on the issue.)

My sophomore classes were all interesting and I finally figured
out how to get better grades on my tests. Some teachers quizzed
you not on course content, but on the things covered in their
'outside reading' lists. Others graded you based on the 'exact
wording' of the concepts discussed in class, to make sure you
had really listened, understood and made precise notes.

Two colorful classroom events stand out in my memory. One occurred in the Grand Lecture Hall of the Chemistry Department.
With great personal pride, the Department Head...Fr. Fiekers...
unveiled what he called—"The World's Largest Periodic Table".
Spanning most all of the lecture hall's wide front wall and
running almost to the high ceiling, it was made up of 18-inch-
square ceramic tiles...one for each of the 96 then-known atomic
elements. (When we later wrote our Senior Musical satirizing
college life, we celebrated Fr. Fiekers grand accomplishment
with a song and dance number titled—"I've Got The Biggest In
The World.")

An equally memorable event took place in the Biology Department Lecture Hall. As we entered, we saw a draped object on the long lecture table. With glee, the white haired Department Head, Fr. Busam (affectionately known as Bunny Busam), whisked away the covering to reveal a skeletal torso. With enthusiastic pride, Fr. Busam declared—"Here it is, Gentlemen! I've been waiting for 20-years to actually get my hands on a female pelvis!" As we roared with laughter, Fr. Busam at first looked confused, and then realizing what he had said. He turned a very bright red...a nice contrast to his black cassock.

By today's standards, humor like this no-doubt seems pretty lame. But it was considered "pushing the envelope" at Holy Cross in 1954.

❖ ❖ ❖ ❖

Thanks to Holy Cross's relatively small size, I could get to play a fairly large role in some of the activities that I enjoyed most. I joined the Dramatics Society, played a few minor roles, and began designing and building stage sets. I replenished my high school stage makeup kit and took on that role as well. (To earn a little extra money, I also did freelance stage makeup for some of the local amateur productions at the Worcester Women's Club and elsewhere.) And with the help of a few friends, I designed and built our Sophomore Class entry in the annual Homecoming Weekend display competition. We won, with a huge papier-mâché figure of the Colgate 'Red Indian' Mascot plunging over the falls in a canoe to his destruction. All this led to an expanded role over the next two years in building Homecoming displays, doing the decorations for all the formal dances, and designing and staging our Senior Musical. Little did I know it then...but all this extra-curricular stuff would lead directly to my future encounter with Mentor Number 2.

❖   ❖   ❖   ❖

NROTC Summer Cruise #2—
It actually wasn't a cruise at all. We spent most of our first month at Camp Lejeune in North Carolina...where we trained in amphibious warfare. Climbing down cargo nets from troop ships anchored offshore, we'd board WWII-era plywood landing craft and storm the beaches in full-scale armed assaults. We'd repeat this again and again in all kinds of seas and all kinds of weather, until it became second nature and our assaults overwhelmed the defending enemy. Between times, we'd perfect our rifle marksmanship at one of the Base's many firing ranges.

One month later, we deployed to the Naval Air Station in Corpus Christi, Texas for an added 3-weeks of training. After several days in the classroom and various hangers, and practice in both parachute and ejection seat simulators, we finally went up in two-seater fighter aircraft...where the pilots did their best to scare the Bejesus out of us with triple rolls and free-falls. Unlike our cruise the year before, this time they bunked all of us from Holy Cross together in the same barracks. This added greatly to the camaraderie...and certainly to the hijinks.

Our last night in Corpus Christi, they announced that after chow we could depart for home at midnight, rather than wait around for dismissal the next morning. Bill Sullivan and I quickly checked the Greyhound schedule and booked a 2:00AM bus to Houston that would get us in just before 7:00AM. From there, we planned to hitchhike 350-miles to New Orleans for some R&R...and then on to Kessler Air Force Base in Biloxi, Mississippi...where we hoped to get a free plane hop home. We changed quickly into sport shirts and khakis, packed our duffels, and took the Base Bus to the local Greyhound Terminal. But our little R&R side trip turned into quite an odyssey.

It took rides from four different drivers to get us to New Orleans and then Biloxi. One was with a raving self-styled preacher, who kept pulling over to ask us to "Repent!" Another was with a grim farm family, who for some reason pulled away while we were still in a gas station rest room. (Fortunately, they tossed out our duffels a short distance down the road.) Another was with a scary looking guy claiming to be on parole, who pressured us for a cash payment as we were pulling into New Orleans. We pleaded poverty and got away unharmed. By then it was close to 10:00PM. We checked our duffels at the bus station and headed directly for the French Quarter. After a few hours slaking our thirst, downing some Po-Boys and oysters, and enjoying some jazz, we decided it wasn't worth the money to book a hotel. The benches at the bus station would do just fine. We snoozed there a bit...but some raps on our feet brought us fully awake. The New Orleans Cops just didn't buy our story that we were waiting for a bus, and sent us on our way. So we headed to a pew in St. Louis Cathedral in Jackson Square. Being regular churchgoers, we were fairly experienced in the art of dozing off in a kneeling position, but the fact that the Cathedral's pews were made of cast iron and not wood made those occasional head bumps a bit painful. Finally, sun up occurred. So we headed off for a breakfast of beignets and chicory coffee at the Café Du Monde in the French Market, before heading out to the highway for our final leg to Biloxi.

We stood in the sun on that sweltering highway for over two hours before a car pulled over to pick us up. Why it took so long we later learned was because the local media had been warning motorists that a pair of serial killers was in the area. Remarkably, it was 3 girls in a red Caddy convertible who offered us the lift. Either they thought we looked harmless, or hoped to make headlines by bringing us to justice. Kessler Air Force Base was about 90-miles east, and they took us right to the front gate where the guards waved us in after chatting up the girls, who they seemed to know.

After showing our documents at the Base Administration Office, we were given a double room in the BOQ (Bachelor Officers Quarters). After a much needed shower and shave, we dressed in our uniforms and headed off to the mess hall...and before heading back to our room for some long overdue sleep, went to Flight Operations to sign up for a flight that would take us to or close to New York. The best we could get was two days away.

Ten hours later, a phone call awoke us...with an alert that all available aircraft had been ordered to fly out immediately due to a fast approaching hurricane. They said we could get a flight north if we got to a particular hanger within the next half hour. Otherwise we'd probably have to wait a week or more for a flight north. We ran to the hanger, only to find that there was now just a single slot available. Bill and I flipped a coin. I won, grabbed a chute, hopped on a jeep, which sped to a B-25 Bomber that was already on the taxiway. Someone opened the hatch and lent me a hand to help me aboard...all just seconds before takeoff.

The B-25 was a twin prop WWII vintage aircraft with a distinctive Plexiglas nose that in wartime housed the bombardier. (The Doolittle Raiders used B-25s to bomb Tokyo in April 1942.) Because all of the 6 crew seats were already taken, I was told to crawl through the nose hatch and effectively play bombardier for our flight north. But rather than manning a bombsight, I'd be using a map book to do visual sightings of various towns and landmarks along the way to aid the navigator. And so I did, for our entire 1,400-mile flight to Rome, New York. (Only about 120-miles distant from my home in Green Island.)

The journey was truly amazing! Lying prone on my stomach with an unobstructed view, I felt like a soaring hawk. The transitions from hills, to valleys, to flatlands looked from this height like a heavily rumpled blanket strewn across my boyhood bed. The rivers and lakes with their dozens of tributaries glistened like silver. The fields and pastures of the many farms looked like a patchwork quilt of different colors. And the cities and towns and the smoke-billowing factories looked like tiny toy miniatures. We've all looked out of plane windows at the ground below. But being able to look straight down and have an unobstructed panoramic view for hours was an experience not to be forgotten. However, this did not come without one instance of fear. As we landed for a refueling stop about midway through our flight north...and as I saw the ground rushing up toward me...I held my breath praying that the nose wheel held!

During the time I was flying north, Bill remained stuck at Kessler, where nothing would be flying out for several days or more. Ultimately, he had to travel to NYC by train. A few weeks later I visited him at his home in Mineola, NY, where we compared notes and prepared for our return to our Junior year at Holy Cross.

❖   ❖   ❖   ❖

Junior Year—
Bill and I moved into a better room in a different dorm and got back to our studies. As Juniors and Seniors we would all be taking double course levels in Philosophy, per the Jesuit tradition. As a result of this concentration, many of the bull sessions and much of the humor among all our classmates would center around these somewhat arcane studies.

My involvement in building things picked up significantly. For our Homecoming Week display competition, I built a giant Archimedes in his bathtub...a 24-foot figure reclining in a 16-foot tub...memorializing Archimedes' "Eureka" moment when he discovered the principle of water displacement. The caption read—"*Archimedes Saved Syracuse in 213BC...But Nothing Can Save Them Now.*" We won the display competition, but sadly lost the football game to Syracuse!

My next project was heading up the Decorating Committee for our Junior Prom, which was always held in the Campus Field

House... a 147' x 200' space with a 20' high ceiling...that was once an old airline hanger before being dismantled and moved to Holy Cross. Until then, Prom decorations in the Field House were pretty basic... drapery hung walls, a few big banners, and 40 or so round tables with centerpiece decorations.

This time, with a work crew of six classmates, we transformed the space into a 'Gatsby-style' Garden Party at a Long Island Estate. As couples entered and looked up, they saw a midnight blue sky with thousands of twinkling stars...while an illuminated moon slowly traversed the heavens on a diagonal path. The dance floor was rimed with rose entwined railings...with brightly lit Japanese lanterns above. The raised bandstand was tented with swaths of colorful silk fabric.

As party-goers turned back toward the entrance, they suddenly realized that they had entered the Garden through the French doors of a massive 145-foot wide Mansion. Using stage scenery techniques, we had completely surfaced the façade of the Field House's tiered balcony section to simulate a 1920s vintage Long Island great house...with a sloping red-tiled roof, complete with lighted dormers. And at the far end of the Garden, there was a grotto for taking pictures. Lush with potted trees and flowering plants, it featured a cascading waterfall and a pool stocked with flitting goldfish. Predictably, some of our classmates swallowed a live goldfish or two, to the shudders and giggles of their dates! (Incidentally, while Holy Cross was a 'dry' school, formal dances were the one exception. Ice and 'set-ups' were provided at every table, and the couples brought in their own preferred adult beverages.)

The Prom proved such a huge success that my team was asked to decorate all of the formal dances for all classes right up until our graduation. To give us a proper workspace, we were given keys to a large basement area in one of the dorms. This quickly became our nightly clubhouse for the next 18-months. We could escape 'lights out' and convene there to work...or just to schmooze.

My increasingly odd hours presented a problem for Bill, who liked to go to bed early, as he still does. We finally came up with a grand bargain. I'd leave our room by 10:00PM and quietly tiptoe back in late at night, without turning on the lights or disturbing him. In exchange, he'd let me sleep in, until right before my first class at 9:00AM. This meant that he'd check me in at daily Mass. It worked because Bill rose early to serve the 6:00AM Mass for Fr. Hart in the Jesuit residency, and was therefore exempted from attending the 7:00AM Mass in St. Joseph's Chapel. Per our 'sleep hours' agreement, after serving the 6:00AM Mass, he'd then take my assigned seat in the Chapel for the pre-Mass check-in...and then quietly slip out before the Mass began. Of course, I should have attended daily Mass...and would have liked to. But getting there by 7:00AM was far too early for me!

As all this was going on, several of my friends were talking about restoring an old Holy Cross tradition dating from the 1930s... writing and staging an original Class Musical. We all thought this was a great idea, especially because one of our classmates...Peter J. Matthews...was a brilliant pianist and composer with a flare for contemporary satire and musical theatre. I agreed to design and stage the musical, which we'd call—*"Up At Seven"*—and premiere it during Parents Weekend in our Senior Year. As you'll later see, that decision ultimately proved life changing for me!

It was right up there with another major decision that I made at the very beginning of our Junior year. Along with Bill and several of my other classmates, I opted to switch into the NROTC Marine Corps program. In that program, our Holy Cross military courses would be taught by a very inspiring USMC Lt. Colonel named J. F. Donahoe. And at the end of our Junior year, our summer training would take place in Quantico, Virginia. Then upon graduation, I'd be commissioned as a Second Lieutenant in the U.S. Marine Corps.

If you're counting, this makes the fourth branch of the Armed Forces for me...Army, Coast Guard, Navy, and now Marines!

❖ ❖ ❖ ❖

Quantico, Virginia—
I was very Gung Ho when I got to Quantico, and that continued for more than a month. But my boyhood asthma and allergies, that had never been a problem before, now seriously affected my performance. So great was the problem that my eyes actually swelled shut during one of our 20-mile forced marches through the Quantico hills. Added to that, was the fact that I was far less conditioned than the other Midshipmen who had played sports throughout high school and college. At Quantico, I found myself always lagging behind on the obstacle course and long runs. This was, of course, very obvious to our Marine trainers.

So they pulled me aside and scheduled me for a comprehensive physical exam. The result was that they officially "washed me out" of the Marine program. They gave me the option of either going directly home, or remaining with my unit in Quantico for the balance of our scheduled summer training...but with administrative rather than field duties. I opted for the later and worked in the Base Office, scheduling unit-training events. But now, being detached from the action, my Gung Ho enthusiasm more than just faded...it totally evaporated, making me wonder what I was ever thinking of, in signing up for the Marines!

❖ ❖ ❖ ❖

Senior Year at Holy Cross—
When I returned to campus, I found a note to report to Lt. Colonel Donahoe ASAP. My assumption was that by 'washing out' at Quantico I had lost my NROTC scholarship. But apparently that was not the case. The Navy Department had notified the Lt. Colonel that Quantico had absolutely no authority to dis-enroll me, and that I was to officially remain in the program until my pre-commissioning physical the week before graduation... which, of course, I would fail. Recognizing this, the Navy further notified the Lt. Colonel that I should be "given the opportunity" to restore my enrollment in the Navy option, where I would most assuredly meet the physical requirements. I asked the Lt. Colonel what he would do in my situation. His response—"*I'd tell them to go screw!*" Liking that advice, I opted to not request reenrollment in the Navy program. The result? I remained on a full NROTC scholarship through graduation...and after graduation could immediately begin my civilian career because I no

longer had that 3-year military service obligation. But what about the Draft? It still existed. However then, under the 'Reserve Forces Act', it required only 6-months of active duty. Of course, I'd be a lowly private. But 6-months was a lot better than 3-years!

❖　❖　❖　❖

With Parents Day fast approaching, we moved into high gear, readying our Senior Musical *"Up At Seven"*. Rewriting scripts, rehearsing song and dance numbers, building sets, blocking movements, finalizing all the costumes and props, and promoting the show to make sure we had a full house for its several performances. Finally we were ready for Opening Night...and it proved to be a smash hit! The 2-plus-hour show satirized student life at Holy Cross and skewered more than a few sacred cows. But I had no idea on how significantly it would affect my future life. Because it was this Show that brought my second Mentor into my life!

One night after the performance, a classmate's father invited a few of us out for a late dinner. I was seated next to him, and after chatting for sometime he asked me if I had ever considered going to work on Madison Avenue. I was a little confused, assuming that he meant somehow working in retailing at one of the big stores in New York City. He laughed and explained that by "Madison Avenue" he meant 'the advertising business'. He was the head of J. Walter Thompson's Chicago office. JWT was probably the country's biggest ad agency at the time...and he said they were always looking for talented young men and women.

111

When I told him that I was a Chemistry Major and knew next to nothing about advertising, he said—"*Even better!*" And then explained that J. Walter Thompson had *Shell Chemical* as a major client...and that a person with a Chemistry Degree was exactly the kind of person that both the Agency and the Client needed.

When he offered to set up an interview and tour for me at JWT's headquarters in NYC and at Shell Chemical's offices a few blocks away...I figured 'why not'...it'd be fun and educational. Plus, who could resist an all-expense-paid visit to New York City. A few days later, we confirmed the dates and arrangements.

J. Walter Thompson occupied several floors in the Chrysler Building on 42nd Street. When I arrived at 10:00AM, a Senior VP greeted me in the reception area and introduced me to the Account Supervisor on the Shell Chemical account, who would tour me around. After an impressive multi-media presentation in a large conference room, we visited several departments...creative, account service, media, market research, sales promotion... where each supervisor briefly described their department's role in the whole process, and the work that each did. Then after lunch in the Agency's impressive dining room, we walked over to Shell Chemical, where I met the Advertising Manager, who explained how Shell and the Agency worked together.

All this was an astonishing revelation! These people were actually paid to do those things that I loved doing! Until then, I had always assumed that I'd be working 9-to-5 for some Chemical Company, making a living in sales or some other aspect of marketing. And only on nights and weekends would I get the chance to enjoy all my creative avocations...but only as an unpaid hobby. However, in advertising I could have it all...all at the very same time! What a great career! It was definitely going to be Advertising for me! From that moment on, I decided I wanted to be what they were then calling...an "Ad Man".

And there was a compelling second reason. My career would be in New York City...the place where I most wanted to live. While my classmates would no doubt have fine careers in the Chemical Industry, they'd be home-based in places like Michigan, Delaware, Louisiana, or Texas...or at one of the company's many sales offices around the country. But I'd be in NYC..."The Big Apple"...the most exciting place on earth!

In 1957, the recruiters from nine separate Chemical Companies came to Holy Cross seeking to fill positions in sales, plant operations, and research. I interviewed with them all, asking only about possible positions in their Advertising Departments. A few said they'd find out and get back to me. That resulted in invitations from two companies...Union Carbide and Shell Chemical... to come to New York for interviews. Separately, I applied to a few major Advertising Agencies. Only my contacts at J. Walter Thompson asked me to come back for a formal interview.

All of these interviews went well and resulted in job offers from all three. Even though both Union Carbide and Shell Chemical named a starting salary of $5,700 (about $110 a week, which was top dollar back then for a BS Chemistry grad)...and JWT paid only a flat $35 a week in their Training Program...I leaned toward the Agency, assuming that was the best place to learn the ad business.

While still mulling my options, I happened to meet a girl copywriter from another big ad agency at a St. Patrick's Day Party in New York. When I told her about my offers, she strongly advised taking one of the corporate positions. She said that when an Agency gets a new account, they almost always want to staff it with someone who has industry experience. The people in their Training Programs get overlooked again and again...and either remain stuck in the mailroom or given a very junior position. She advised putting in a year or two on the Client side, making good money while learning the business, and then being 'that guy' with industry experience that an Agency is anxious to hire. This made great sense to me, so I took the offer from Union Carbide.

So as you see, that out-of-the-blue unplanned dinner, hosted by a classmate's father...with his confusing-to-me question—"*Have you ever considered going to work on Madison Avenue?*"—sent me on a career path that I would never have even conceived of without him. And though we were together for only a very few hours... he ranks as one of the four true Mentors in my life!

❖   ❖   ❖   ❖

Stupidity Confessed—
On a November afternoon in 1953, while still a Freshman, I made a decision so stupid that I could have died that very day... and none of the things reported in this memoir from that day forward would ever have occurred. My grieving parents would

have claimed my body and I'd be laying in our family plot in Troy, NY. Gone...and by now, totally forgotten.

On that November day, a group of us were gathered in the off-campus rooms of two of our classmates, with lots of booze and laughter. There was a big campus stag dance that night in the Field House and our Freshman Prom was a little over a month away. I had just phoned a girl back home and she said she'd come to Worcester as my date for the Prom. I was happy about that. But then I realized that I could really use some extra cash for the tux and flowers and a few extras. This brought to mind the stunt that my high school friend, Bill Mahoney, had just pulled while pledging at his Yale fraternity. He bet $75 that he could down a full fifth of scotch that night and still sing their fight song. Bill won that $75.

Well, stupid me! Eyeing a pint bottle of "Graves 100-proof Gin", I bet my friends $50 that I could down it all in one sitting. The bet was on...and I poured the gin into a pitcher, added some ice cubes, and whispered the word "vermouth". Swirling around the world's largest martini, I brought it up to my lips and 'chug-a-lugged' the whole thing down within seconds. I had no idea that I had just ingested a lethal dose of ethyl alcohol! Apparently, that much alcohol, consumed that fast, almost always results in an immediate coma, followed by cardiac arrest. (Some years later, the Boston Globe reported on the death of a sailor who had consumed a half-pint of gin in less than one hour. The many friends who knew of my unlikely survival, were quick to point out how totally stupid I had been.)

Needless to say, I survived. But my next recollection after that first half-hour was awakening in my dorm room the following morning. I felt fine, with absolutely no hangover. But apparently...with the help of my friends...I had made it back to my room, showered and dressed, and attended the Stag Dance where I did some impressive steps on the floor! (I can only assume that I had gotten very sick somewhere along the route to expel some of the lethal potion.)

I've certainly done other stupid things during the course of my life. But this stands out as a red flag warning. What seems a fairly small decision, casually made, can have a profound impact. The consequences can prove nonreversible...and maybe even fatal. Think hard before you act!

❖ ❖ ❖ ❖

REFLECTIONS
—on my college years—

What a difference four years can make!

It all began with the assumption that I'd be on active duty in the Coast Guard until age 25. But after pivoting to the Navy, and then again to the Marines, I ended up with no military obligations and the freedom to start my civilian career four years sooner...at age 21.

It also all began with the assumption that my lifelong career would be in the Chemical Industry. But instead it became Advertising.

How did that all happen? I credit three things...Holy Cross... Unplanned Events...and most of all...the Mentor who opened my eyes to possibilities that I would never otherwise have even imagined—

<u>Holy Cross provided the perfect environment-</u>
- A true Liberal Arts education...and not just a narrow science degree.
- A college small enough to let me play an active role in all the many creative activities I loved most.

- A culture that encouraged good behavior...free from 'Party School' distractions.
- An exemplary group of fellow students...to grow with and to learn from.

Unplanned Events-
- That unexpected evening session at the Coast Guard Academy...where I learned that resignations by Academy Graduates were not being accepted.
- Keeping my NROTC/Holy Cross option open...even after entering the Coast Guard Academy.
- Choosing the NROTC Marine option...unwittingly erasing my military obligations.
- That unplanned dinner with a classmate's father who became my next Mentor...

My Mentor-
- While our time together was certainly brief, he opened my eyes and then opened the doors to my lifelong career in advertising... amazingly impacting the course of my entire future life.

And I should probably add one last thing about timing—
This was the 1950s, well before the Baby Boom. As such, good jobs were plentiful, with far fewer new college grads competing for them. Also, there were none of the Student Protests that so disrupted college campuses in the 1970s. (Younger friends, who were Social Activists in the '70s, tell me regretfully that they had effectively wasted 10 years of their future adult lives playing hippie radicals.)

❖ ❖ ❖ ❖

Views I held strongly at age 21—
- I would make New York City my permanent home.
- I would make Advertising my lifetime career.
- I felt ready to meet the many challenges of both.
- Though always being blessed with good fortune, I knew that it would take far more than good fortune from now on.

And the negatives I carried with me—
- I had led a pretty sheltered life until now.
- I had no idea how big business actually worked.
- I had no family friends or personal contacts in NYC.
- I had never before encountered and dealt with truly serious culture shocks.

❖ ❖ ❖ ❖

New York City

June 1957—

As I made my way uptown to begin my first day at Union Carbide, I couldn't help but reflect on the fact that I was now the newest member of a group of nearly 7-million people tying to earn their living in New York City. Did that put me at the end of the long line, or at the front? It was the front, of course!

Union Carbide's headquarters was at the corner of Madison Avenue and 42nd Street, right in the heart of Manhattan. And my apartment...which I shared with 3 other guys...was right in the heart of Greenwich Village, at W. 8th Street and MacDougal. This was before Greenwich Village became a major tourist destination. It was still home to bohemian artists, writers and avant-guard creative-types. Our apartment...a fourth-floor walkup over *Sam Kramer's Jewelry Shop*...was a summer sublet, owned by two professors who were traveling abroad. It had features rarely found in an apartment back then—an espresso maker, a hi-fi component system, a working fireplace, and rooftop access providing a sweeping view north to the Empire State Building and beyond. Two of my Holy Cross classmates... John LaFontaine and Lenny Szumiloski...and John's high school friend, Kevin Reardon, had found the apartment and were looking for a fourth roommate to share expenses. When John heard I too was going to be working in New York, he asked me to join them. I did! Thus, the four of us began our New York careers and adventures together!

Matter of fact, each night after returning from the office, we'd gather in the apartment over drinks to compare notes and plot our grand ploys for the next day. Our inspiration was the satirical British handbook—*One Upsmanship*—which became a Terry Thomas movie and later the musical—*How To Succeed In Business Without Really Trying*. We'd pick an 'admirable quality' that was sure to impress our bosses. Maybe it would be "frugality" for tomorrow...then "compassion" the day after... and then "efficiency" the day after that. Once agreeing on our 'admirable quality' for the following day, we'd then all set out on our missions at our different companies. After work, we'd then compare notes on the specific ploys we had employed and the reactions of our bosses. If all this seems devious, despicable and mischievous, it probably was. But in our defense, we only picked good qualities that actually made our efforts on behalf of our bosses stronger.

After our evening drinks and strategy sessions, we'd start to prepare dinner. We had divided up the tasks, and mine was the cooking. Usually things weren't ready until 8:30 or so...but being fast eaters we were ready to head out by 9:00PM.

Living in the Village in 1957 was fabulous. A particularly favorite haunt of mine was *Café Figaro*, about 3-blocks south on the corner of MacDougal and Bleecker Streets. Opened only the year before, it was an unpretentious coffee shop where patrons sat around, sipping espresso and smoking pipes or Gauloises cigarettes...while quietly discussing philosophy and cultural issues. The walls were papered with vintage sheets of LaFigaro newspapers, and the lighting was dim. (A few years later, *Café Figaro* gained fame for its celebrity clientele that included Jack

Kerouac, Alan Ginsberg, Lenny Bruce, and later Bob Dylan, Sam Shepard and Al Pacino.)

Jazz legends performed nightly in Village Clubs like the *Village Vanguard*, the *Half Note* and the *Five Spot*. Theolonious Monk, Charlie Mingus, Gerry Mulligan, Dave Brubeck and George Sheering were among our favorites. Some nights we'd go to *Marie's Crisis* to hear Cole Porter tunes. Or to the cozy *Hotel Earle* on Waverly Place, where British pianist Laurie Brewis played and sang show tunes...usually with the help of the audience, many of whom were Broadway performers between engagements.

Among the great local bars were the *White Horse Tavern*...a hangout for writers and artists (Dylan Thomas used to drink there)...and *Julius's Tavern* (better known as '*Dirty Julius*', thanks to the 2-inch-thick dust clinging to the rafters and hanging lamps.) Both were popular with the gay community...and all the rest of us...who enjoyed their 15¢ beers and 50¢ burgers.

That first summer, I saw my first Broadway Shows...*Westside Story*, *The Bells Are Ringing*, and a few more. You could buy last-minute standing-room tickets for just $15. And I saw my first ballet and my first opera in the old *Metropolitan Opera* House at 39th and Broadway. Life in New York City sure beat Green Island, Troy and Worcester!

What about work? That too was great. As one of the world's leading chemical companies, Union Carbide exemplified the style and class of big business during the Eisenhower economic boom years. And even as a rookie, I found myself in the center of it all. Sixteen other new college grads joined the company in New York the same month I did. All but for me were assigned to the Sales Department, working at 'correspondent desks' in a big open space on one of the lower floors. In that time before the internet, they manned telephone lines that were directly linked to the Company's many regional sales offices...answering questions about product availability, pricing and delivery... and booking, confirming and tracking orders. In contrast, I had a private office in the Advertising Department on an upper floor. And on just my second day on the job, I was called into a meeting to be given a special assignment.

The hugely influential book *"The Organization Man"* had stirred quite a debate in the Executive Suite. The book reported a dramatic shift in American values...with more and more employees strongly preferring to be part of an organizational team, rather than to work as empowered individuals. In sharp contrast, Ayn Rand's magnus opus *"Atlas Shrugged"* argued that innovation and true progress comes only from individual achievement... and not from organizational 'group think'.

Well, it appeared that Union Carbide was about to launch a major effort to recruit 'the best and the brightest' from colleges and universities around the country. The question was...should they emphasize the opportunities in being part of a truly amazing organization (à la *"The Organization Man"*)...or should they emphasize the opportunities for unlimited individual achievement (à la Ayn Rand)? Upon learning that they had a recent college grad in their Ad Department who had just been exposed to the recruitment efforts of their major competitors...a person who presumably also had a first-hand understanding of the aspirations of today's students...they somehow thought that I should be given the assignment of spearheading their recruitment promotional efforts—the brochures, presentations, mailings and advertisements. After a briefing with top management, I was introduced to the various account teams at the corporation's Ad Agency, Promotion Agency, and PR Agency...officially becoming "their client" at age 21. And amazingly...all this had occurred during my first two weeks on the job!

Not surprisingly, I thought that emphasizing the 'individual' was the way to go. And it turned out that the corporate executives and all the agencies felt that way too. So we had smooth sailing.

Managing the program was a tremendous learning experience...the meetings, the presentations, tracking the schedules and expenses. All new to me. But exhilarating!

A month or two later, I was tasked with supervising the set-up of a relatively small trade show exhibit in the old Coliseum on Columbus Circle. (I was astonished to learn that our 20-foot-by-3-foot booth cost more to build than the current worth of my family home in Green Island...and that we had to pay staggeringly high fees to have three separate trade unions replace a single burned out light bulb in our exhibit. A far cry from the papier-mâché and chicken wire Homecoming Week displays we built at Holy Cross!)

This led to my being tapped to set up all of the Chemical Division's trade show exhibits, and to manage the related hospitality suites in the convention hotels. That took me to Philadelphia, Biloxi, New Orleans, Chicago, Los Angeles and San Francisco, among other cities. There I met and worked with the Company's local sales people and joined them in entertaining some of their biggest customers and prospects.

In hindsight, I was learning that business success was not just about making and selling superior products. It was about developing personal relationships and negotiating agreements. People skills that they don't teach you in the classroom!

I stayed at Union Carbide for five years before moving on to an ad agency. During those years I learned a tremendous amount about marketing and all facets of advertising and sales promotion...thanks to a series of job promotions and new assignments that I received about every 9-months. In my third year at Union Carbide, our department was reorganized and we were assigned to work directly with the product management teams serving various industries. This broadened my industry experience significantly. And equally important...in working directly with top executives, brand managers, the sales force, customers, suppliers and prospects... I was able not only to develop management skills...but also presentation and consensus-building skills. Again, all valuable things I had never learned in college.

How important was my BS in Chemistry? Without it, I would never have been hired by Union Carbide. So in that sense, it was very important. And it put me in a starting-salary class far above what I would have received as an ad agency trainee. But how important was it on the job? It was important only in that it let me say..."*I don't understand*"...without embarrassment when learning about the effective uses of one of our products. Guys without a chemistry background would often try to fake it...missing out on getting an in-depth understanding of our product's full competitive advantages.

Outside of work, I took a few evening courses at NYU...one in "Business Writing", another in "Direct Marketing". My professor for the latter was Fred Messner, an advertising executive who some years later recruited me to join a new division at McCann-Erickson. 'Who you know' is sometimes almost as important as "What you know".

Another truly formative event was when the very influential Douglas McGregor of the University of Chicago asked Union Carbide to be the test-site for his breakthrough "*Management by Objectives*" concepts...and that our Department was selected as the site for his test. Basically, the program redefined the classic roles of 'managers' and 'subordinates"...with managers becoming facilitators rather than dictatorial bosses...and subordinates being fully-involved in the decision-making process of how best to achieve an agreed-upon objective. Needless to say, this changed the dynamics tremendously, as McGregor's team effectively muzzled our red-faced bosses and encouraged we workers to spout out our ideas and feel free to criticize current management practices. Nothing was to be considered off-limits; and no idea was to be summarily shot-down or squelched. After a few uncomfortable weeks, the power of this new management approach was clear to see. And in fact, in years following it became the model for effective management countrywide. It also made it second nature for me to volunteer my ideas and suggestions without first being asked...and to be far less 'political' in my dealings with higher-ups.

So much else happened during my five-years at Union Carbide, that things are best described by category rather than chronology. So here goes, starting with the most important—

Anne—

New Years Eve, 1957—The average person makes hundreds of little decisions a week...most all of them so inconsequential that they require virtually no pre-thought. But every now and then, one of these little decisions can make a profound impact on your entire future life. And that indeed was the case with a spur-of-the-moment decision I made on the morning of December 31, 1957. Because without making it, I would never have met Anne Elizabeth Hibbard...the love-of-my-life. The remarkable woman who would become my friend, my soul mate, my wife, and the mother to our four wonderful children.

That New Years Eve morning, I was still back home in Green Island celebrating the Christmas Holidays with my family, when my New York City roommate John LaFontaine called to tell me that they had just decided to throw a New Years Eve party that night in our big new apartment. It sounded like fun, so I quickly decided to grab the late morning train from Troy to Grand Central Station. There wasn't time to call around for a date, so when John offered to call his high school friend Selma Quinn...who was a student nurse uptown at Columbia Presbyterian Hospital

School of Nursing...to see if she could bring along another girl for me, I said "Great". Then I quickly packed, hugged my parents 'good bye' and headed off for the train station.

For the past three months, our new apartment at 15 W. 84th Street had become something of a 'Party Central'. Right off Central Park West, it was in a classy 8-story building with a doorman. Our fully furnished apartment featured a 35-foot long sunken living room. On the higher level, we had built a bar clad entirely in green malachite Formica. And after much testing, we made the 'Side Car' our official house cocktail. John rented a piano and I donated my Bongo drums.

As soon as we moved in, we discovered that most of the other tenants were single women...secretaries, flight attendants, and corporate trainees...sharing apartment expenses. And indeed, they quickly made us feel welcome! We became especially great friends with the four southern girls living in the apartment directly below ours. Recent grads from the University of North Carolina, they were all new to New York City. (A few years later, John and Fran were married. Theirs was the only romance between we eight!) As our circle of friends grew exponentially... from work and friends-of-friends...it was not uncommon to find 50 or more gathered in our apartment every evening. Often, I'd go to bed around 1:00AM with the partying still going strong.

But back to that New Years Eve—After a quick bite at a local coffee shop, I reached our apartment about an hour before the party began, just in time to change and help with the set-up. Selma Quinn arrived early with her date, Frank Bulkley.

(Actually, they were secretly married. It was kept a secret, because back then student nurses at Columbia Presbyterian were not allowed to marry.) Selma and Frank brought along a second couple, whom I had never before met...along with the 'blind date' that Selma had recruited for me. This 'blind date' definitely wasn't Anne! Anne was the one with the other guy—a tall, good-looking, young Resident Doctor at Columbia Presbyterian Hospital.

It took me less than 10-minutes to realize that my 'blind date' and I were about as compatible as oil-and-water. So I wandered off to chat with our other guests for the rest of the party. That left my 'blind date' to zero in on Anne's doctor escort. I looked admiringly at how well Anne handled the situation, but we never spoke after the brief introductions when she first arrived.

Valentine's Day, 1958—The Nursing School was holding a Valentine's Day Dance and Anne was the dance chairman. Selma suggested that Anne invite me to the dance, but Anne said she'd probably be too busy to have a date, plus she hardly knew me at all. But Selma insisted...saying that Anne and I "were made for each other". (Fifty years later, in thanking Selma for bringing us together, I reminded her of that quote. Looking perplexed, Selma said—"*Gee...to be honest I used to say that to everyone. It was just a casual expression. And I don't really remember saying that to Anne!*")

But thanks to Selma, Anne did invite me to the dance, and I attended. It was a nice evening, but little more.

Mononucleosis—About two months later, I found myself in the old Midtown Hospital on East 49th Street, with a diagnosis of Infectious Mononucleosis. Because I had a big presentation coming up at the office, I had ignored my fever and night sweats for over a week. But when I finally went to the Company's medical department and they saw I was turning jaundiced, they escorted me directly to a local doctor who diagnosed me as having mono. And when he learned I shared a single bedroom with three other guys, he insisted that I be immediately admitted to Midtown Hospital in a private room. Union Carbide arranged it all.

I phoned my boss to tell him what was up...and he responded by having all the papers in and on my desk boxed up and...along with the full four-drawer metal filing cabinet in my office...delivered directly to my hospital room the next morning. He said this would keep me occupied, and was far better than sending flowers! Somehow, I wasn't amused and never did open the boxes or the filing cabinet.

I also phoned my roommates, asking them to drop off some of my clothes, my mail, a few books, and my little TV. (Back then, hospital rooms didn't have TVs.) They said they'd try, but there were a few parties coming up. Suffice it to say, they never did come.

Day after day, as I lay in my room absolutely bored, finally something magical happened. Through the door came the lovely Anne...smartly dressed, with heels and stockings, a pillbox hat, a small purse and white gloves. She asked how I was, she sat and we talked and talked. I was overwhelmed with her kindness in coming to see me. It meant more than you could ever

132

know. This was a woman unlike all others. I knew it then. And I still know it today!

Years later Anne told me that she was very hesitant in coming to see me. But it had been Selma again who assured her that "we were made for each other". It may have been just a throwaway statement, but in our case it proved to be absolutely true!

I finally persuaded my doctor to let me go home to Green Island where I could recuperate with my family. Our doctor up there believed a high dose of antibiotics could quickly knock out mono, and that seemed to work for me. So after two weeks of treatment, I was able to return to New York and my job. Once back, I immediately, called Anne to ask her out for dinner and a show. This was the first real 'adult date' I had in New York. City. Up until then, it was all parties and fun outings as a group. I asked if she had a favorite restaurant, and she recommended *"The Champlain"* a little French bistro at 115 W. 49th Street. There she introduced me to escargot and steak au poivre. I loved them both. After dinner, we went to see a Broadway Musical at the NY City Center. As the chorus began singing about statehood, I asked Anne what State they were singing about. When she reminded me that the musical we were seeing was called "Oklahoma", we laughingly agreed that maybe I was not as fully cured as I had thought.

From then on, it seemed that we could not get enough of each other. And New York City in the late 1950s was a glorious place for romance and courtship. By this time, Anne had graduated from Nursing School...earning her BS from Columbia and her

RN...and had begun working at Columbia Presbyterian Hospital. We spent as much time together as we possibly could. But I knew that before long I would be drafted...separating us for a full two years.

When I first started work at Union Carbide, the Army's "6-Month Program" was still in effect. But I had delayed signing up for it because you could gain seniority, plus a year-end bonus, if you put in a full year with the Company first. Then without warning, the "6-Month Program" option was cancelled. And now I was facing a two-year stint as an Army draftee.

In late July 1958, the letter finally arrived...declaring me '1-A'... and ordering me to report to the *Armed Forces Examination & Induction Center* in lower Manhattan for a pre-induction physical, followed by immediate mobilization.

I bade Anne and my roommates goodbye, informed my bosses, and reported as ordered the following week. While jammed in a huge hall with other draftees, a sergeant called out—"*Anyone here ever have heart disease, venereal disease, or mononucleosis?*" When I raised my hand, he asked—"*Which ones?*" And then—"*How recently?*' My answer—"*Just Mono, three months ago.*"...got me sent immediately to Governors Island in New York Harbor for 3-days of monitored tests. The result? I wound up reclassified as '2-A'...which meant temporary rejection from the Draft. So miraculously...I remained a civilian...and Anne and I were not separated.

Jumping ahead in this story...we became formally engaged in December 1958 and were married on September 19, 1959. A few months later, the Army cancelled my '2-A' status and re-classified me as ineligible for the Draft, because by then I was an expectant father. Thus...if you're following my unorthodox military career...I had somehow totally avoided any post-college military service!

A word or two about Marriage—

Anne and I were married when we were both 24. And our marriage lasted for 64 years, until her passing at age 88. Over the years, people have often asked me what it takes to have a happy marriage for that long?

The simple answer is that we loved each other dearly and completed each other fully. But that question really deserves a more complete answer. So please bear with me as I offer you my views about marriage. In fact, here's what I'd tell to a young couple considering marriage today—

Without doubt, the decision to marry and the decision about who to marry is arguably the most important decision in your life. Because it begins with an—"*until death do us part*" vow of commitment. And that's difficult—because it's certainly true that over time, people can change and can grow apart. Yes, there's divorce. But divorce comes with a large measure of emo-tional and financial turmoil...along with a profound impact on any children you may have. And if you're a practicing Catholic married in the Church, you know that after divorce you're not free to marry again. It's a one-time-only event.

135

So the compelling physical and emotional attraction we call "love" is not really enough for one to say "yes" to marriage. There are other consequential factors to weigh. Together, you'll be making decisions about where and how to live, about children, finances, careers, life goals. And together, you'll be facing potential setbacks and hardships like income loss, family tragedies, health issues and more. None of us can predict the future and how we'll react to it. But we can and should assess our contrasting decision-making styles and egocentric natures. Do we see things the same way...or do we often agree-to-disagree? Do we share the same moral values? And are there any early warning signs that might suggest issues of dishonesty, irresponsibility, infidelity, or minor and major addictions.

They say that opposites attract. (But over time they can also repel...if the two-forces grow out of balance.) And they also say that "he" marries a girl, thinking that she'll never change. While "she" marries a guy, confident that over time she can change him. While "love" often masks and minimizes all these potential concerns, they should be carefully weighed and addressed before saying—"*I Do!*".

In my view, the three most basic questions to ask yourself before marriage are—"Am I willing to selflessly devote my entire life to the care and happiness of this other person?" "Are they capable of making that same commitment to me?" "Is this the person I want as the co-creator of my children...the one whose genes they'll carry...and upon whom their successful upbringing will depend?" If you can honestly say..."Yes" and "Yes" and

"Yes"...you've likely got the right person to share your future life with!

❖   ❖   ❖   ❖

Even though Anne and I felt we were highly compatible and anxious to marry, we followed the traditional path between courtship, engagement and marriage. We met and spent time with our respective future families. Time with Anne's identical twin sister Barbara, her mother and father Ray and Dorothy Hibbard, and her grandmother Mrs. Agnes Duffy...all of whom lived in Teaneck, NJ. Also time with Anne's aunt and uncle Paul and Frances Duffy, their son Anne's cousin Bob Duffy, and Anne's great aunt Alice Murray. And while in Green Island visiting my parents George and Ann Warner, we spent time with my aunt Irene Peasley and my uncle Joseph Teson. We also visited with Anne's uncle and aunt Ronald and Alvina Hibbard in Troy, where Ronald ran a CPA practice. Happily, we all enjoyed each others company...and Anne and I were warmly welcomed as new members of our respective families.

To show proper respect to Anne's father, I followed tradition and formally requested his approval to ask for her hand in marriage. We met at *Whyte's Restaurant* in downtown New York, near his offices at American Agricultural Chemical Company. Of course, we both knew why we were there...and he said "Yes" without grilling me about my prospects. He then ordered another round of drinks, and we settled into a most pleasant lunch.

We posted our banns and attended Pre-Cana instructions at the church where we planned to be married...*The Church of the Epiphany* in Cliffside Park, New Jersey. And the Hibbard's hosted an engagement party at their home in Teaneck. Unfortunately, my parents couldn't attend. My father was ill and eventually succumbed to his ALS affliction on January 6th, 1959...just weeks after our engagement party. He was just 58 years of age.

At our Wedding on September 19th, 1959, my best man was my close High School friend Bill Gardner; and Anne's maid of honor was her identical twin sister Barbara. My Holy Cross roommate, Bill Sullivan, was there too. Earlier that year, we had arranged a double date between Bill and Barbara. At the time, he was a Marine Officer stationed in Quantico, VA. They too happily fell in love, courted and were married on September 9th, 1960, soon after Bill returned to civilian life.

Our Wedding reception was at the Hibbard home, and after the festivities we drove off in our new Volkswagen Beetle to Albany, where we spent our first night as a married couple at the De-Witt Clinton Hotel. Next day, we drove on to Sainte-Agathe-des-Monts in the Laurentian Mountains north of Montreal, Canada. We stayed at the historic Laurentide Inn. Ten days later, we returned home to our new apartment in Palisade, New Jersey... thrilled to be embarking on our life-journey together!

During our engagement, Anne and I searched for an apartment in Manhattan. But based on our budget, all the places we saw were terrible...small, dark, and dirty. I had been living in a great apartment, splitting expenses with three other guys. Anne was sharing a beautiful Hospital-subsidized apartment overlooking the George Washington Bridge. But once married, she'd have to give it up. Even with our combined incomes, our New York City options looked pretty grim.

Then a fellow-employee at Union Carbide called me. He heard that I was getting married and looking for an apartment. He said that he and his wife were about to leave their great apartment just across the river, close to the Palisades. It was a fully furnished apartment on the top floor of a beautiful Victorian home. The woman owner had originally converted it into an apartment for her son and his wife. But when they were transferred to California, my Union Carbide co-worker and his wife took over. Now they were moving into their first house and the apartment would soon be available. While it was in New Jersey, it was only a 20-minute bus ride to New York's Port Authority Terminal. He invited Anne and I to dinner to see the place and meet his landlady.

It was perfect! We met the lovely owner and on-the-spot decided that this would be our first home. It was cozy, spotless, had great views, and we could park right outside. And the rent was so affordable that we could buy our first car...a new, black Volkswagen with a list price of $1,649. That would be the car that would carry us in style to our honeymoon destination.

While we were engaged, Anne decided to specialize in Public Health Nursing, so that our future work schedules would better coincide...with no night and weekend assignments. But that meant that through much of our engagement period she would be taking her required graduate school courses during the daytime, and work as a private duty nurse at Columbia Presbyterian Hospital on the 4:00PM to Midnight shift.

While it might sound crazy...and would only work in a "never sleeps" city like New York, I would pick her up at midnight and we would then go out for dinner, dancing, a movie, or whatever until 3:30 or 4:00AM. To make that work, I'd come home from the office around 6:00PM...grab a bite and rest-up until 11:00 or 11:30PM. Then I'd head up to greet Anne, as her Hospital shift ended.

No longer living with the other guys, I had moved into a furnished room in an elderly couples' apartment very near the Hospital. Knowing that I would soon be married, I had decided not to sign a new 3-year lease with the guys...and I had a better option!

One of Anne's former patients had been asking her to come live with them. She declined, but said that her fiancé needed a place to stay until they were married. It all worked out, and I moved into a cozy room in their apartment on 185th Street just off Broadway. The rent? $15 a week...which included breakfast and them doing all my wash. When I said the breakfasts were getting much too hearty for my appetite, they suggested I have dinner with them instead. What a deal! I remained with them until our apartment in New Jersey became available...just two weeks before our wedding. I then moved all my stuff in to get the place settled. Meanwhile, Anne had accepted an offer from the *Visiting Nurse Service* of *New Jersey* and had moved back to her parents' home in Teaneck to prepare for the wedding.

<u>Starting our family</u>—We didn't have too long to wait! In a little more than nine months after our honeymoon, Matthew was born. And 17-months later, Barbara was born. And 21-months later, Peter was born. (Christopher would come nearly nine years later.) Thank heavens that Anne was such a capable, caring, highly skilled nursing professional...quickly becoming a full-time mom to three lively tots...and a loving wife to a totally inexperienced 'only-child' husband.

Sadly, Anne's father Ray lived to see only Matthew...his first grandchild. He died of a heart attack on December 19, 1960 at age 56.

Our Palisade apartment had only one bedroom, and we knew that we'd need something bigger before Barbara was born. That led to our first house...a small Cape Cod, much further out in Washington Township, NJ. Priced at $17,000, we could just afford it, thanks to our small savings and being approved for a big mortgage. We moved into our new home in August 1961, and stayed there for seven years before moving to a far bigger place in Ridgewood, NJ. At age 25, we now owned our first house! And our first mortgage!

❖   ❖   ❖   ❖

As homeowners and new parents, we enthusiastically embraced the traditional roles that nature and tradition assigned us. Me as the "Daddy"—primarily responsible for providing a safe and secure home for the well-being and happiness for our growing family. And Anne as the "Mommy"—primarily responsible for running our household and assuring that our precious children were cared for in the best possible way. We decided on this so-called "division of labor" because it let us take full advantage of our particular strengths. As a Nurse, Anne had the professional skills <u>and</u> the temperament to nurture and care for what would eventually become our four children. (To be blunt—in both of these areas, I was basically clueless!)

But I did have the best earnings potential. I was on a fast-track with a major corporation and I had just received a nice raise. While Anne could have worked as an RN at a local Hospital or Medical Facility, we didn't really need a second income—and neither Anne's mother or mine were in a position to help out with the children. Plus, we really relished the idea of "playing house"...with me as "breadwinner" and Anne as "stay at home" Mom. This worked out very well for us!

❖   ❖   ❖   ❖

There are so many stories I could tell you about the joys and challenges we had raising our four children to young adult-hood. Telling you all that would require hundreds of extra pages and would fall way beyond the scope of this book's focus on decision-making. But permit me to make a few reflections as I look back—

- By far, the most creative thing an individual can ever do in this life is to create another human being. And Anne and I were blessed to be able to create four.
- It's astonishing just how different...but how alike...four

children born of the same parents and raised in the same house can be. But that's a wonderful thing, because it expands family life exponentially. With each child bringing to the family new perspectives, new interests, new talents, new friends and more.

- There are lots of "how to" books on childrearing. Unfortunately, many of them result in unintended and unfortunate consequences. We raised our children like we were raised… never micro-managed, domineered, or essentially ignored to do whatever they darned well pleased. Our parents set clear standards that we tried to follow to earn their love and praise. They let us make our own decisions about our activities, friends and more. Saying "no" only now and then. But reprimanding us whenever we did something unkind or harmful to ourselves or others. And above all, they spoke to us intelligently as family members…not as "know-nothing" kids or subordinates. We were happy children and turned out all right…so we followed that same approach with our four. I think it worked!

- I only recently remembered something my Mother said to me when Matthew, our first-born, arrived. *"Remember, you don't own your children, God loans them to you to raise for Him. You're privileged that He trusts you so greatly with their care!"*

- Our children come to us as helpless newborns…and then leave us as independent adults. But the bond of love between you remains forever!

❖   ❖   ❖   ❖

143

Bosses—

During my 5 years at Union Carbide, I had a number of excellent bosses...with one notable exception. His name was Ed Hannigan (changed here for legal reasons) and he was in charge of the Company's print advertising campaigns and, as such, the prime liaison with our ad agency. My friend and future business partner, John Bicking, had been Ed's assistant. But for reasons too complex to detail here, John went to our Department Manager with a "him or me" transfer request. John was reassigned to the Sales Department and I was appointed as Ed Hannigan's new assistant.

As I went to Ed's office for the very first time to say hello and express my enthusiasm after being told of my new assignment, I waited in Ed's doorway while he completed a phone call. I was more than a little shocked when I overheard him say—*"Yes, I know that new directory ad was replete with errors. It was the fault of my new assistant. It's not the first time he's screwed up. I'll be taking corrective action. It's a guy named Jack Warner."*

As he turned in his chair, Ed spotted me in his doorway. And with a big smile, invited me to come in. He offered no explanation. Though I was shell-shocked by the event I said nothing. But I bit down so hard on my pipe stem that it literally snapped off in my mouth! (Later that month in my annual Human Resources evaluation report, the single negative comment was that I "had the bad habit of entering a supervisor's office without knocking.")

While chapters could be written about Ed Hannigan's questionable ethics, he certainly was a charmer. Always a big smile and a warm, upbeat personality. He could weave a story to keep you spell bound, and leave you with the impression that he was both remarkably caring and extremely talented. But all that was a façade. He was always "dealing from beneath the deck", to win the pot from others!

Two early incidents stand out—

The first was when Ed told me he was flying home to visit his sick mother in Butte, Montana. He said he had to make sure her Will made him her sole heir, cutting out his two wastrel brothers and a sister. On his return, with a smile and a wink he said—"*Mission Accomplished.*"

The second was one afternoon when he shared his personal philosophy about money, which he called…"A Tolerance for Ambiguity"… the ability to live and enjoy a future life before it actually happens. For example, he said, that each year he would take out a personal loan in anticipation of his yet-to-come raises. This let him live next-year's lifestyle without waiting. It let him, as he described it—"live the future now." If all this was intended to educate and transform me, it really didn't. To me it was what I'd simply call—"dancing on the edge".

But those were the very least of his doings. Over the next several months, Ed assigned me a number of projects, which I later learned were intended to keep me occupied and in-the-dark over his more questionable activities. They were 'make-work' assignments with no useful purpose. And while I knew the team at the ad agency from my prior work with them on the Company's recruitment campaign, Ed never once included me in any of his meetings with them. I'm certain that was to head-off any repeat of the Bicking "blowing the whistle" situation.

But in all fairness, the projects Ed assigned me ultimately did prove valuable by increasing my skills and broadening my experience. I conducted market research studies and hosted focus groups...did in-depth analyses of alternate media buys...developed and tested alternative message strategies...and more. Ed complemented me on my work. But as I later learned, all my final reports were simply filed away...and never acted upon or shared with anyone inside or outside the Company.

Then one day, out of the blue, word spread that Ed had just submitted his resignation. He gave two-weeks notice, but applied his accrued sick days to cover that two-week period. He bade us all goodbye, as he gathered up his personal belongings to head off to his great new job, which would begin that very next day.

Ed had landed a VP Account Supervisor position at a top NYC advertising agency on one of their major consumer product accounts. Impressive, in that Ed had no prior consumer product or TV experience and had never before worked at an ad agency or supervised more than a single person...namely, Bicking and then me. But he was a charmer...and a very quick study! And I instantly realized why he had all those books on 'Brand Management' and 'TV Production' and 'The Clio Awards" in his office over the past few months.

Even before Ed left the building, I was called into the Department Manager's office and told that I was being promoted to take over Ed's position. That afternoon, when I moved into Ed's office and opened the file drawers, I was stunned to learn the extent of his fabrications.

In a thick file labeled "Jack Warner", I found a series of monthly reports to management on the training I was supposedly receiving...planning sessions with the agency...responsibilities being turned over to me...job ratings and progress reports that were presumably reviewed with me. None of these ever happened! It was all a complete lie!

In a file marked "Ad Copy", I found the original ad copy created by the Agency...along with the retyped versions all showing Ed as the copywriter.

In another file labeled "Ad Readership Studies", I found the original reports from the various magazines we advertised in... and the revised reports submitted by Ed to Management. Consistently, he raised our ad readership scores by double digits.

Why Ed hadn't purged all these from his files before leaving, I'll never know. And I certainly never kept up with him to ask!

So what happened? I called the Agency to tell them I was the new Ad Manager. They expressed relief and shared their concern over what they called Ed's "unorthodox management style". I told them that Ed had intentionally kept me in-the-dark, so I had lots to catch up on with them. They suggested a morning meeting the next day to get things rolling.

Perhaps I should have told Management about Ed's fabricated reports on my training. But I didn't...rationalizing that I was next-in-line for the spot anyway, and that I had the skills to handle it. Was that an ethical lapse? Probably "yes".

❖ ❖ ❖ ❖

As I took on my first management job, I soon realized two things—

1. Up until then I had always been given individual project assignments...things to do and complete. Now, it was my job to figure out 'what needed to be done'.

2. I was now a boss, with an eager new assistant named Harley, fresh out of college. It was my job to train him and to develop his skills...along with motivating him to deliver the greatest productivity.

Thankfully, both challenges went well. And Harley and I were eager to take on more responsibilities...as the Ad Department reorganized along Product and Market lines. As mentioned earlier, this had us work directly as part of the Marketing teams in several areas. And as such, deliver the full range of marketing services...print advertising, sales promotion, direct mail, trade shows, publicity, etc.

❖ ❖ ❖ ❖

Decision Time—

Life was good at Union Carbide and I had no real complaints. I had received a steady stream of nice promotions and salary increases, but admittedly things were becoming a bit routine. Also, I still had in mind my original plan...to one-day move up to an ad agency...and I was well behind schedule. That's when the call came in!

Fred Messner, who had taught the Direct Marketing course I had taken at NYU, phoned to say there was an opportunity that might interest me at McCann- Erickson. Fred was now a VP at McCann's newly formed ITSM Division. (He explained that ITSM stood for Industrial, Technical & Scientific Marketing.) The Division was formed to service Exxon Chemical (then still called Enjay) and other major industrial clients. It was a fee-based, full-service agency...doing everything from advertising, to sales promotion, to direct marketing, to technical literature, to public relations. They were building a team of experienced people and were paying top dollar. One of my former Union Carbide co-workers, Bill Fenwick, had already signed on. (More about Bill later.) And they'd like me to join the team. In all, they planned to build an initial staff of about 30. The starting salary? Twice what I was currently making at Union Carbide.

It may surprise you to know that I agonized over the decision. McCann-Erickson was one of the country's leading ad agencies. Exactly the type of agency I hoped to one-day join. But my

longer-term prospects were pretty great at Union Carbide...
where I had an excellent relationship with upper management.
If I stayed, I could no-doubt have a wonderful lifetime career
with the Company...likely climbing the corporate ladder to a
highly paid senior position. Conversely, there was little to no
security in the agency business. Staff churn was frequent. You
could make it big, or find yourself out on the street, as clients
came and went. Things could be exciting, but gut wrenching
too. What to do? What to do?

Then a stupid little accident resolved things for me. That Sunday
morning as I sat on the living room floor with work papers spread
about, I knocked over my almost full cup of black coffee. Even
after sopping it all up and using carpet cleaner, a tell tale brown
stain remained. Anne said, not to worry: she'd call the carpet-
cleaning guy the next day. But alas, his diagnosis—"Sorry...we
can't get stains out of rayon carpets." We had, of course, been told
by the realtor that our carpet was genuine wool.

So there I was, looking at the stain and worrying that buying
new wall-to-wall carpeting would definitely blow our budget...
when a little voice in my head said—*"Stupid! They're offering
you twice the money. You're an idiot not to take it!"*

Well, the very next morning I called Fred Messner and told him
I'd be honored to join the ITSM team. That was initially the <u>very
worst</u> decision I ever made. But without it, I would never have
made the <u>very best</u> business decision I ever made!

❖ ❖ ❖ ❖

REFLECTIONS
on my early
New York City years

As a kid, I always joked about moving to New York City "to make my fame and fortune." The fame and fortune part hadn't yet happened, but everything else was pretty terrific!

As a career, the advertising field perfectly matched my interests and talents. Which meant that I found my work almost always challenging fun. Never repetitious, never a burden or a drudge. Satisfying in its variety. Project oriented—which provided a true sense of accomplishment on a frequently occurring basis... as each project was completed.

The people I worked with were great, with an exception or two. The Corporation was Grade-A. And the City in the late 1950s and early 60s was a dazzling cornucopia of excitement, culture and commerce.

And best of all, I wasn't here alone! I now had a family. An astoundingly wonderful wife, two remarkable children, and our own little house in the suburbs. Love abounded! And we were just getting

started. Anne and I were 22 when we first met. Now we were 26...
with hopefully more children and 60 or 70 years before us!

❖   ❖   ❖   ❖

By now, you might be thinking that I've been uncommonly
blessed with enormous good luck. That I've always seemed to
be in the right place at the right time. Met the right people. And
that all the paths I've chosen seemed to have worked out to my
advantage. How could this be? Why is that so?

Ruling out some form of Divine Intervention, I come back to the
belief that much of what we call "good luck" is really just the
result of earlier good decision-making, based on harnessing all
three of these decision-making resources that were described
earlier in this book—

- Intuition—based on all your earlier life experiences that
  have fine-tuned your "gut feel" to size up a situation, person,
  or opportunity. In other words..."Does it really feel right?"
- The Experiences of Others—studying and learning from both
  the *positive* and *negative* 'role-models' provided by those who
  have faced these decisions before. In other words..."What
  are the pitfalls? Where can you go wrong? What's needed to
  make it work right?"
- Mentors—seeking out and carefully listening to those wise
  elders who can open your eyes to new possibilities...or alter-
  natives...that you might never have known of or considered
  before. In other words..."Is there a far better way?" A way
  that will be truly life-changing? A "Eureka Moment"!

And to that...I can add a few more "how to get ahead in business and life" suggestions, based on my first five years actually on the job. At least they've worked for me—

1. Listen, Watch, Absorb—Opportunities and pitfalls are out there everywhere. Don't be so self-absorbed or self-confident that you're somewhat oblivious to their very existence. Take everything in...and form carefully drawn conclusions and guiding principles. Discern where opportunities exist.

2. Keep your eye on your ultimate life goals—and don't let difficult bosses or situations or setbacks demoralize or sidetrack you.

3. Stay Positive—Stay optimistic. Take a break now and then to recharge.

4. Make it...don't fake it—Just the opposite of the advise often given to high-tech startups...where they promise big, well in advance of their ability to actually deliver on their promises. Do the work. And let its proven effectiveness demonstrate your ability to deliver. It's results that matter!

5. Perfect your People Skills...not just your Performance Skills—Whether it's your subordinates or superiors...your customers or prospects...your colleagues or competitors... your parents or children or spouse... you'll achieve far more by asking and listening, with respect and empathy, than you'll ever achieve by simply telling, ordering or demanding. Also use what I call "verbal jitsu" in response to confrontational

153

hostility. Respond with warmth and empathy, rather than a tit-for-tat verbal escalation. It often so disarms the aggressor that their own emotional outburst turns itself around to restore reason to the dialog.

Most all of these things have worked for me. So I pass them along for your consideration.

❖   ❖   ❖   ❖

And one last point about good luck...about being in the right place at the right time. I was not the only one in Brother Anselm's class at La Salle. I was not the only one to hear that Coast Guard Commander tell us that all his fellow Academy grads were still on active duty. I was not the only one at that dinner with a Holy Cross classmate's father who told us about careers in advertising. I was not the only guy to meet Anne at that New Years Eve party. All of us had an equal opportunity to choose the paths flowing from those situations. Or to simply ignore them.

My point is that in life, we're presented with countless potential opportunities. Some big, some little. If we keep our eyes and minds open to recognize them...a few will coalesce to form viable paths leading to our next stage in life.

If we take that path and it works out, we call it "Good Luck". If it's a dead end or worse we call it "Bad Luck". If we ignore it and don't take it at all...we never know where it leads. It's a "nothing'" And we'll probably forget all about it.

So in the final analysis, our luck...either "good" or "bad" or "no-luck-at-all"...depends on the decisions we make! As many before me have said—*"We make our own luck."*

❖ ❖ ❖ ❖

<u>Views I held strongly at age 26</u>—
- I've made the right career choice...Advertising.
- I've made the right romantic choice...Anne.
- I'm now more than ready to make my move to a big Ad Agency.
- Tomorrow will be even brighter than today.

<u>Negatives I've carried with me</u>—
- I was in no way prepared to cope with the cut-throat, high-pressure, roller-coaster world of life in a big New York City Ad Agency.
- I had no real experience in caring for a growing family, raising children, or owning a home.

❖ ❖ ❖ ❖

P.S.—It seems I've mentioned a lot of 'drinking', so far in this book. But it was what you'd call today 'social drinking' and never really got out of hand. Bachelorhood was like that in NYC in the late 1950s. And in business too.
Those days are a very long way behind me!

McCann-Erickson

Spring 1963—

McCann-Erickson was the country's third-largest ad agency, with a client list including Coca-Cola, Exxon (still called Esso back then), General Motors, Nabisco, Citi-Bank, Coors, S.C. Johnson, and dozens more. Under its "wonder-king" chairman, Marion Harper, the agency had just begun its expansion to become Interpublic...with dozens of divisions spanning all fields of marketing, and a network of offices that would operate in over 120 countries. The legendary ad man, Emerson Foote, had just agreed to come out of retirement to become the agency's new president.

McCann's offices were right on Madison Avenue...so in a symbolic sense, I had finally arrived at the place and in the industry that my second Mentor had awakened me to. But while McCann was only a few blocks distant from my old offices in Union Carbide's new headquarters tower at 270 Park Avenue...it was, as I quickly learned, like being transported to a far distant planet. A planet with a hostile environment and populated by predatory creatures.

❖ ❖ ❖ ❖

As previously mentioned, I was hired to be part of McCann's new ITSM division...a 'full-service' ad agency being set up to service "Industrial, Technical, & Scientific Marketing " clients. ITSM's initial client was Exxon's chemical division...called Enjay Chemical back then.

My position was called "Copy-Contact". A hybrid position that combined being a full-time account executive and a full-time copywriter. I'd be working directly with Enjay's marketing people...promoting their Butyl Rubber line in all its many applications...tires, electrical insulation, water barriers, footwear, and more. I'd be one of the four Copy-Contact people assigned to Enjay's various product lines. Bill Fenwick, who would soon be joining us, would be another. (Bill and I had worked together at Union Carbide before Bill moved on about two years prior to work at Marsteller, an industrial ad agency.)

When I arrived that first morning at ITSM, there were only two people in the offices...a secretary and the Creative Director. All the many cubicles and desks were empty...with only a few of them suggesting that someone actually worked there.

I introduced myself to the secretary. She showed me my office space. And then led me directly to McCann's 'Personnel Department' on a lower floor...where I was signed-in, given a stack of policy manuals, and processed as a new McCann employee.

Returning to the ITSM offices, I found a note on my desk saying that the Creative Director wanted to see me. He was very cordial and welcoming...but then apologized for 'the little crisis' he was about to toss me. He said we needed a new Butyl Rubber ad ASAP...because ad space had already been booked in four trade magazines and the plates were needed in three days. He added that we didn't yet have an Art Director—and being new himself, he hadn't yet set up any outside relationships with photographers, retouchers, type setters, or engravers. Then with real seriousness he admonished—

"I really hope you can pull this off, because if the publications don't get the ad plates in time, they'll run blank pages labeled 'Courtesy of Enjay'. There'll be hell to pay. Not only with the client...but especially with Paul Funk. And you don't ever, ever want to get on Paul Funk's shit list!"

I said I'd handle it. And after leaving the Creative Director's office, I asked the secretary to tell me a little about Paul Funk. She said—*"I don't want to go there. But just watch out!"*

Paul Funk, of course, was the founder, president and tsar of ITSM! A personal drinking buddy of Marion Harper. And as I later learned, the orchestrator of the financial coup that would make ITSM so incredibly profitable...simply by exploiting the personal weaknesses of the client's Advertising Director.

In a nutshell, here's Funk's scheme—
Enjay Chemical could replace its entire 23-person marketing services department (and the burden of supervising its people) with a "manpower package" provided by ITSM. To staff that "package", ITSM would recruit and hire the industry's very best people... which of course required paying them well above average salaries. That cost would be passed along directly to Enjay, with two mark-ups. 1. To cover the cost of normal overhead and employee benefits, a 50-percent mark-up would be added to the salary budget. 2. To manage the overall "manpower package", the usual 17.65-percent commission would be added to everything...both the salary/benefit package...and to all the

'out-of-pocket' expenditures for media ad buys, production, travel, etc. And of course, everything would be billed monthly in advance.

Compare that to standard agency practices—
Typically, all client contact, program planning and creative services are provided for free. The agency is compensated by a 15-percent commission on the advertising that actually runs... plus a 17.65-percent mark-up on out-of-pocket ad production expenses. Most Sales Promotion projects are billed on a 'fixed-bid' or hourly charge basis. And PR services are usually provided under a monthly retainer fee.

All in all, The ITSM billing plan was at least 300-percent more profitable than standard agency practices for an industrial account! (And with up-front billing, the agency's cash-flow was significantly enhanced.) I have no direct knowledge of how Funk sold this to Enjay management. But I do know that about 11-months after I joined the company, I was told that the Advertising Director's wife had just appealed directly to McCann's president... *"to please free my husband"*...who was reportedly— "holed-up in a mid-town apartment that was kept well stocked with booze and broads by one Paul Funk."

Then a month later, I heard that the enslaved Advertising Director was now in rehab and his spot was being temporarily filled by Dave Thomas...a bright young guy that many considered heir-apparent to the Enjay presidency.

But back to that first day Butyl Rubber ad assignment—

Fortunately, I was commuting into the City with a friend and neighbor named Bill Mostsad, who was an art director at one of NYC's hot agencies. I called Bill, and he said—"No problem!" We created the ad that night. We had a photo shoot the next day. And he had his agency get the ad plates made for me by the next morning. (Back then, print ads were actually copper engravings nailed to wooden blocks that were secured into a publisher's flat bed printing press. You needed a separate plate for each publication, unless there was time to transship them around.) So with Bill's help, I was able to meet my deadline, putting in a chit for expense reimbursement... which ITSM gladly processed, and passed along to the client with its 17.65-percent mark-up.

❖ ❖ ❖ ❖

It was two more days before I actually met Paul Funk. I heard a booming voice shout out... "WARNER", which I had been told was his preferred way to summon you to his office. Once there, I saw him standing by his desk with Fred Messner, his VP who had hired me. Fred said there'd be a staff meeting that afternoon to introduce everyone on the ITSM team to one other. Funk said nothing, but his appearance told me a lot.

Paul Funk was short. Fortyish. A bit pudgy. Lifts on his heels. A dark blue suit with a solid blue tie. An expression on his face like he had smelled something really bad...as he silently eyed me up and down.

The afternoon staff meeting was one I'll never forget. There were 19 of us present. Funk asked the four account supervisors to tell us in turn about their backgrounds and experience. And throughout, he'd tear them apart...with sharp criticisms, personal insults, and heartless ridicule. Even the nastiest Drill Sergeants at Quantico never went that far with new recruits! Why Funk decided to do this...and even more significantly... why these clearly-experienced account supervisors just sat there and took it, still amazes me. Basic human instinct, manly courage and personal dignity should have required them to either resign on the spot...or to 'cold cock' Funk for the bully he was. But they just sat there red-faced and took it!

In contrast to humiliating the four account supervisors, Funk never said a word or offered a criticism to the rest of us...as we introduced ourselves and reviewed our backgrounds. For some reason, his venom was focused exclusively on the account supervisors. Perhaps tellingly...he never told us a single thing about himself or Fred Messner.

For a time, I suspected that all this might have been a staged opening act...to establish that Paul Funk alone was our 'supreme leader'...and that no challenge to his authority would ever be tolerated. But he repeated it again and again. Every time we had a new campaign for a client, he'd insist that the account supervisor in charge do a full dress rehearsal in front of the agency's assembled team, prior to the actual client presentation. And each time, he'd tear the account supervisor to shreds...while never offering even the slightest aside or criticism to the rest of us assembled.

Against this background, there was a steady stream of... "WARNER" commands, beckoning me to his office...where he'd ask for a status report on a particular program, and more often ask probing questions about client relationships. I knew, of course, why Funk was asking me...and I assume others...these questions. It was apparent to all of us that our productivity and work-quality for Enjay was sub-par...and Funk wanted to see if the client was beginning to complain.

It was no mystery as to why we were delivering so poorly for Enjay. We toiled in a joyless workplace for a cruel and repulsive tyrant. We could look for another job, but that would mean a big sacrifice in salary. So many of us felt trapped by our own avarice. Thus, all the enthusiasm, satisfaction, and camaraderie necessary to do above-average creative work was totally missing at ITSM.

And if that were not enough, there was a second...and even bigger... reason for our poor performance—Funk was diverting a significant percentage of Enjay's "manpower package" into developing new business for the agency. He had brought on a 'rainmaker' and his secretary to find and court new clients. This led to a growing number of speculative presentations... consuming more and more of the staff time that was presumably 100-percent committed to and paid for by Enjay.

To cite my own personal situation—One of the agency's biggest new business prospects was 'Norton Abrasives'... with headquarters in Worcester, Massachusetts (home to Holy Cross). And with one of their bigger plants in Green Island, New York (my boyhood hometown). Learning of this, Funk put me on the Norton account team...not to do any creative work, but there only to establish client rapport. This meant that every Thursday night for 6-weeks, four of us would drive over 200-miles to Worcester...attend multiple client input meetings all day Friday...then drive back home Friday night...rarely getting back before midnight. Beyond that, I had to do considerable background research on the abrasives markets and Norton's competitors to not look like a dummy in the meetings. All in all, during those 6-weeks, a full 30-percent of my work time was diverted from Enjay. Not to mention, having to spend two nights away from my family each week...just to be non-contributing window dressing for a prospect.

Obviously, Funk believed we could get away with shortchanging Enjay and other clients. I know that to be true, because I once overheard him telling Fred Messner—*"An account is secure... even if two-thirds of their staff people want to fire you...as long as you make them believe that you have a close personal relationship with their top management."* Pretty cynical!

What effect did all of this have on me? Considerable! Almost every morning in the shower before heading off to work, my heart would start palpitating faster and faster...and I'd often feel nauseous. Through my mind would race a series of questions. What had I done? Why did I leave a successful spot in a great corporation...where I could do satisfying work, and feel both appreciated and rewarded? And all for what? To say I was an "Ad Man" on Madison Avenue? Just for the money?

Increasingly, I found myself seriously wondering if I was really cut out for the agency side of the business. Asking myself if I should maybe regroup and go back to the corporate side. But after a long weekend of quiet reflection, I finally concluded that the problem was not the ad agency business itself...it was McCann's mismanaged ITSM Division. And that I should not let the aberration they called ITSM taint my whole view of ad agency life.

After all, I had found working directly with clients a rewarding pleasure. The Enjay people were great to work with...just like the people I had worked with successfully at Union Carbide. And they respected my observations and recommendations, viewing me as an expert in my field. I especially enjoyed our extended travel times together...to out-of-town industry conventions, field offices, and to meet with their customers. All in all, I loved in-depth client work!

Then, thanks to a 3-day McCann-Erickson account service seminar, I finally learned how a successful agency should operate. Bill Fenwick and I were invited to attend a special gathering of about 30 account executives and account supervisors from various McCann divisions and locations. The purpose was to share ideas and methods to better serve our clients. The session was held at the 'Deep Hollow Dude Ranch' on Long Island. This was where Teddy Roosevelt trained his Rough Riders...and for some unexplained reason it was owned by McCann-Erickson's parent company, Interpublic. The other attendees were all terrific guys. Smart and talented, warm and friendly, funny and self-deprecating, and above all, willing to share. Between sessions and after hours over drinks, I'd ask them how their groups were organized and the inner workings of their operations. All in all, this 3-day meeting was...for me...a post-graduate course in how to run a successful ad agency!

Bottom line—I was in the right field...just in the wrong place.

That's when I started to take seriously my friend John Bicking's frequent suggestions that we start our own ad agency. John had left Union Carbide 4-years before and was the assistant ad manager of National Distiller's 'US Industrial Chemicals' division. He was doing a bit of freelance with a guy who was running a one-man agency, and I helped out with a little freelance of my own. But I wasn't ready for a move that big, because I had a growing family and only modest savings.

Anne, Matthew, Barbara and I were still living in Washington Township when Peter was born in 1963. We had just expanded the house by adding a second floor dormer. That chewed up a good bit of the extra money we had. In contrast, John and his wife Marilyn were both working and had no children. So for me...money more than courage was the issue.

On the plus side, I did have good contacts with some potential clients...Ad Directors at several chemical companies that could benefit from the services we could provide. Personal contacts that I had made over the years in my membership in the "Chemical Advertisers Group", while I was at Union Carbide. And all of us were still members of the venerable and tightknit "Chemists Club" on East 41st Street.

❖　❖　❖　❖

But it was two notable events that finally persuaded me to move ahead—both of which convinced me that I should permanently distance myself from Paul Funk and employers like him. While starting a new ad agency posed great risks, I'd be in control of my own destiny. With my time, talents, and livelihood no longer subject to the priorities of questionable employers.

Event Number 1—ITSM was conducting an important test market for Enjay, designed to determine if various "Home & Garden" specialty-chemical products could be profitably sold in kiosks at Esso Service Stations around the country. To manage the effort, ITSM brought in an experienced account supervisor who had handled the Texaco account at another agency. We became fairly good friends, so I knew a good amount about the project.

As time went on, he told me of his growing concern that the test market was becoming seriously flawed. That's because Funk had vetoed hiring a professional firm to audit sales at the Esso Service Station test locations. Instead, he wanted any ITSM employee traveling close to a test site, to simply swing by and do quick sales counts. The result was grossly unreliable data. Some of the ITSM 'audit takers' weren't sure if there were 6 cans, or 12 cans, or 24 cans to the case. Some visited only a few of the many locations...or just made up all the data because they were running late and didn't want to admit they had violated Funk's directive.

The expression is—"garbage in, garbage out"—and that's exactly what we had.

So how did Funk handle it? He eliminated any hard data in the agency's final report. In his live presentation to Dave Thomas and Enjay top management, he reported only vaguely generalized results...all qualitative fluff, rather than specific quantitative sales results. Their reaction? *"This isn't what we asked you to find out. We're not paying you a penny for this useless report."*

Two things happened on the afternoon of that presentation. My friend, the ITSM account supervisor, was fired...and as he feared, all the blame for the botched test market was heaped on him. And then, an hour later, Funk yelled out—"WARNER!"

When I arrived in his office, he thrust a piece a paper in my hands...saying—*"This concerns you."* It was an internal memo announcing my promotion to become the new account supervisor replacing my just ousted friend. I nodded 'thank you' and headed for the door. But Funk stopped me by shouting out—*"If you screw up, I'll cut your balls off!"* That brought me to a standstill. And before I could turn around to face him, he added—*"Your first assignment is to get me all my money for that test market project that you're now in charge of."*

Minutes later, back in my office, I called Dave Thomas to tell him I was now his new account supervisor. He laughed and said—*"Good luck with that!"* I knew Dave pretty well, and our relationship had always been very good. So I leveled with him—

"I've been following the test marketing program pretty closely, and I couldn't agree more that the report you received didn't come close to delivering on its objectives. But I think there are some pretty useful findings in the raw data that are probably worth digging into and not loosing." He agreed, and suggested we get together for lunch the following day...which was a Friday.

At the lunch, together we mapped out a list of specific questions that we'd like to see answered. I told him I'd work on it over the weekend, and we agreed to meet again late Monday morning. As we parted, Dave said something quite amazing. He said—*"You know, this is the first time since I've been working with McCann-Erickson that I've felt anyone at the agency was actually telling me the truth."*

Back at my office, late that same Friday...I gathered up all the test market files to work with over the weekend...Funk predictably stormed through my door yelling out—*"Got my money yet?"* I answered—*"Working on it."*

Monday afternoon after I returned from my second meeting with Dave Thomas, Funk barged into my office again, and repeated—*"Got my money yet?"*
I responded—*"Oh yes, forgot to tell you...Dave Thomas has just approved payment and will process the invoice as soon as he receives it."* A startled Funk, picked up my phone to call Dave, who without explanation confirmed that yes it was true...before hanging up on Funk.

Neither Dave Thomas nor I ever revealed to Funk why things had changed. And Funk never asked. But from that moment on, Paul Funk treated me differently. It was now a cordial "Jack" and not a snarly "WARNER".

Event Number 2—Two months later, Funk asked me to come by his office to meet with him and McCann's new president. After a little chit-chat, Funk told me they had just signed the Hyster Lift Truck account and had agreed to open a new ITSM branch in Portland, Oregon to service the account. And that they'd like me to go out there to head things up. With it would come a significant promotion and nice salary increase.

I expressed gratitude for the opportunity and their confidence in me...and said I'd discuss it all with my wife and get back to them in the morning. (I of course, had zero interest in moving to Portland...far from NYC, my family and friends, and still then an advertising backwater. Which meant, that if I lost my job out there, I'd likely never get back into the ad agency mainstream.)

So that next morning, I gave them my decision to pass on the opportunity.
Showing his true duplicitous nature, Funk said—"We figured you were too smart to go for it...but it was worth a try."

That cynical comment cemented my decision to put ITSM far behind me!

❖   ❖   ❖   ❖

REFLECTIONS
—on my departure from McCann-Erickson—

As despicable as he was, I owe Paul Funk a debt of gratitude. Because if it were not for him, I would probably have never started my own ad agency. I would have just left ITSM for another agency job. But the Funk experience showed me the downside of working as just an employee...always beholden to the sometimes-questionable priorities and often make-work assignments of others. Better to be your own boss and set your own priorities. That lets you control your own life and your own time. Of course, it also means you have no one to blame but yourself, if you mess up. But that's only fair...and preferable to suffering the consequences of the mess up of others.

And there's more. About six-months before I left ITSM, President John F. Kennedy was assassinated. As the first Catholic to become President, in the very first election I could vote in, I had always followed his career pretty closely. In an early memoir, he had said something that really resonated with me. At the time, I was feeling somewhat overwhelmed by a growing number of business and personal responsibilities...and I marveled at how someone in Kennedy's infinitely more demanding position could possibly cope with all the many and far larger calls for his attention. In his memoir, he gave me the answer. He explained that early on in his career, he realized that at least half of the things he was asked to do led nowhere, or were at best unproductive. Discerning the difference was the key to effectively doubling the time he had to deal with the truly important stuff. Being my own boss would let me do that. Life was too short to waste half of it on go-nowhere stuff!

❖ ❖ ❖ ❖

Views I held strongly at age 28—
- I now had all the skills necessary to do a superior job for most industrial clients.
- It was now the right time for me to open my own ad agency.
- The agency must be New York City based.
- The agency should specialize in providing a full range of marketing services to the industrial and commercial divisions of Fortune 500-type companies.
- The choice of the right partners, clients, and staffers would be critical.
- For the business to thrive, high ethical standards and absolute honesty with clients were musts.

And the negatives I carried with me—
- I'd be starting a business in a field characterized by high-risk and high-volatility.
- I'd never run a business before and had no expertise in the legal, financial and administrative aspects.

- I had very limited financial resources and had no outside investor prospects.
- I'd be starting the business with no clients and no firm commitments from prospective clients.

❖ ❖ ❖ ❖

Warner, Bicking & Fenwick, Inc.

May 11, 1964—

It was now official! We had just signed our incorporation papers at Cliff Chu's law offices in lower Manhattan and were now on the subway, heading north to our new offices at 335 East 51st Street, just off First Avenue. Rather than leasing affordable but second-rate offices in a commercial building closer to Madison Avenue, we had opted instead for ground floor space in a classy residential building with a doorman. Because essentially it was a 5-room apartment, it came with a kitchen and a neat little rear garden. Since we hoped to attract Fortune 500-type clients, we figured that holding relaxed breakfast and luncheon meetings in a garden or living room setting would project our creativity in a way that a run-of-the-mill midtown office never could!

The three of us were equal partners, each putting in $2,000 as seed money. We had no outside investors, so our total capital was $6,000. This would let us pay our rent and telephone service, print stationery and business cards, decorate the place with partitions and display walls that we constructed ourselves, spray paint some secondhand desks and filing cabinets, and rent a few typewriters. The used couches, coffee tables, end tables, lamps, housewares, garden furniture and artwork, were all bought at the Salvation Army or came from our personal homes. All put together, the place looked terrific—from the welcoming "Warner, Bicking & Fenwick, Inc." sign behind the reception desk...to the warm and homey ambience of the 'living room'...to the inviting al fresco 'garden room', where we served clients coffee and pastries or fancy salads on fine china, with sterling silver cutlery and cloth napkins.

All this, of course, left us no money for payroll. So we agreed to go without salary until we could pay ourselves what we were making in our last jobs. Why put in more of our own money, only to have it returned to us as taxable salary? But what about staff? We'd have a few friends 'populate' the place whenever a potential client came to visit. They'd make the place look absolutely buzzing! Also, John's former secretary at U.S. Industrial Chemicals, Jeanne Clifford, who was between jobs, had agreed to join us as "secretary/receptionist/office manager" as soon as we could afford her. Until then, we paid her hourly for the very few hours we needed her each week. Beyond that, we lined up a number of free-lancers for project work. Most important was finding a great art director, and here we were fortunate. Anne's cousin Bob Duffy had a boyhood friend...Rod Capawana...who was hoping to join a good 'start-up' agency in a senior position. It proved a perfect match, and after a few months of freelance, Rod became our first art director, my creative team partner, and eventually WB&F's Creative Director...remaining with us through many years of growth.

So—let me tell you more about my partners and why we thought we could make it together in a very competitive field.

John Bicking had his BS in Chemistry and Communications from Fordham. A brilliant and very hard working guy, he had particular talents in financial management, business administration, and printing and advertising production. These were talents that far exceeded those of the other two of us. Like Bill and I, John had seven-years experience in managing industrial communications programs—but all of it on the client side. He had never worked at an ad agency or handled multiple accounts. John was married to his high school sweetheart, Marilyn, who was an Operating Room Nurse at Englewood Hospital. They had no children and lived in a nice home in Oradell, NJ. John, Marilyn, Anne and I had been close friends for over six years.

Bill Fenwick was truly a polymath, or Renaissance Man, or whatever you call a person gifted in all the academic, scientific and cultural arts. He had his PhD in Nuclear Chemistry, had been a Professor of Mathematics at St. John's University, wrote and produced an Off-Broadway show—with his own original costume and scenic designs. And when married shortly after we opened the agency, he designed and had fabricated the wedding rings, the chalice and the Priest's vestments. He also wrote a special organ arrangement for the wedding's processional... a Bach-version of *"They tried to tell us we're too young"*. And in addition, he designed a multi-tiered chocolate wedding cake for the Plaza Hotel reception...rightly assuming that most everyone would enjoy chocolate over the usual white cake.

At St. John's, Bill had been the faculty advisor to the student "Public Affairs Club" at the time when Fidel Castro first visited New York City to appear at the UN. Castro's newly appointed Prime Minister was with him, and accepted an invitation to speak at the "Public Affairs Club". At the end of that talk, he invited all of the Club's officers to visit Havana to see the changes being made in his Country. Even though the U.S. State Department fully encouraged the visit...because U.S. policy toward Cuba was still under review and the State Department believed the trip might provide useful intelligence...the President of St.

John's threatened to expel any student who accepted the invitation and visited Cuba. Defying that threat, they went anyway. At this point, Bill threw himself into the breach. To protect the students, he drafted an 'expose' criticizing the St. John's administration and documenting the whole incident. And he threatened to release this expose to the *New York Daily News* if any of the students were expelled. St. John's President relented, but only in exchange for Bill's resignation...which he willing gave.

A friend then recommend that Bill leave academia entirely, to take an open spot in the Ad Department at Union Carbide. He did...which is how we became colleagues and friends. We worked together there for 3-years, before Bill was hired away by the Marsteller Ad Agency...where he worked for another 2-years before joining ITSM...bringing us back together.

Bill was brilliant, articulate, creative, and always fun to be with. He had high moral standards and a great work ethic. And like John and I, Bill was a devout Catholic. His equally gifted fiancée and soon-to-be-wife, Kay, was Editor In Chief of "The Catholic Encyclopedia". Until they were married, Bill lived with his sight-impaired Mother and younger brother uptown, in the Washington Heights section of NYC.

❖ ❖ ❖ ❖

What made us think we could succeed as a new ad agency? We would be truly unique...filling a void that other agencies could not fill. Not only would we be offering the broad range of coordinated marketing services greatly in demand by major industrial

companies...we'd also have the technical expertise and corporate marketing experience to work as knowledgeable partners
with their product management and R&D people. In addition,
we had the technical background to communicate persuasively
and empathetically with their customers and prospects.

The need for coordinated marketing services was great. Most
industrial companies had to hire and work with separate agencies and vendors to create and produce their ads, their product
literature, their direct mail, trade shows, PR, sales training and
incentive programs, and more. The result was not only usually
disjointed, but also very inefficient in terms of both costs and
management supervisory time.

WB&F could create and implement a completely integrated
communications program—achieving full synergy in terms
of both message and graphics. And the resultant savings from
eliminated duplication of efforts could be redeployed to fuel far
stronger programs.

At least that was our pitch. And to test it out before launching
our agency, we put on formal presentations to nine of the corporate advertising directors that we knew from the 'Chemical
Advertisers Group' and the 'Chemists Club'. All were extremely
enthusiastic, all but promising to give us their accounts once we
opened our shop. This gave us the courage to move on.

How many of the nine did we ultimately sign? Zero. Nada. None.
All begged off—explaining that they'd have to launch a full-scale
agency review, giving all their existing agencies a chance to

compete...with several of their bosses in on the evaluations and decisions. They added that we should come back to them in a year or so, after we had established a track record as a going concern. Bottom line—no one wanted to peg their careers on a start-up, no matter how good it sounded. No one wanted to go first.

So...Warner, Bicking & Fenwick opened its doors with no clients, which meant no initial source of income. Character building, to say the least! However, we were able to get a friend at Union Carbide to assign us project work in writing and producing their technical data sheets. These we churned out by the dozens as we went around "cold calling" likely prospects.

I must admit that I was entering 'panic mode' as I saw our family bank account shrinking weekly...to cover our mortgage, utilities, food, taxes, and other expenses. But John and Bill stayed buoyant, which kept me going. And gradually, agency income grew. We had vowed not to pay ourselves anything until we could match our previous salaries. And that became possible after nine months in business. I remember that day well, because our personal bank account had shrunk to just $36 on that day of salvation! Yes, I could have requested a salary advance as I saw the agency income grow...or borrowed some bridge money from my mother. But happily, neither was necessary.

Normally, it would take far longer for an agency to become solvent. But we were fee based, not commission based... another distinction. Clients paid us a monthly retainer fee for program planning and client sessions...and hourly charges for implemented projects. All out-of-pocket expenses (including ad space and time) were billed at agency cost, with no mark-ups or commissions. The client savings here usually exceeded our retainer fees...benefiting the client...and of great importance... giving us excellent cash flow.

As we made the new business rounds, we succeeded in adding a few smaller technical accounts—*Isotopes, Inc... Standard Gauge*...and *Victaulic, Inc.* I particularly enjoyed signing *Victaulic*...which was one of McCann-Erickson's oldest accounts and, as such, featured in their Agency Museum on the top floor of their headquarters building. (I wonder what Funk thought.)

But we needed to sign some big "showcase accounts". While we had a number of prime prospects who had told us they loved our concept, we just couldn't seem to budge them. It was the perennial problem of not wanting to take a chance on a new agency before they had a proven track record. We kept calling on our prime prospects so often that we feared we'd actually start turning them off. So we decided to create an outrageous direct mail campaign to summarize our benefit story...and truly demonstrate our creativity.

We designed a 5-part program to run over 5-weeks. Strictly speaking, our program wasn't actually 'direct mail'. Because our target list was just 28 people in 14 companies...and because each piece was very large...we had them all hand delivered, rather than mailed. But whatever you call it, it worked! We signed 6 great new clients within two months!

Our first deliverable was a perfect replica of a giant "Victor" mousetrap (fabricated in our basement with the help of my kids...silk screening the red and blue Victor logo onto 12" x 30" pine boards...and attaching all the authentic-looking, but safe, metal parts.) An origami mouse carried our message about how we could help you "build a better bait", etc.

Another deliverable contained a hand-crafted Wizard's hat... with a message stressing our technical prowess, etc. And the final deliverable was a freshly baked 14" apple pie...with our phone number in icing on the top. The message—"We can help you get a bigger slice of the pie!" A pie cutter, paper plates, forks and napkins were included to encourage sharing around the office...and to get everyone saying..."We should hire these guys!"

Almost immediately, *Chemical Engineering* (a McGraw-Hill Magazine) called to ask us to reproduce the program for them, as a prospecting tool. We said—"We'll give you something even better if you hire us." So they did. The direct mail program we created for them (this time actual mailings to a list of 200+), won the *Direct Marketing Association's* "Best Campaign of the Year Award"...gaining us extensive press coverage and a featured speaking spot at their very well attended Annual Conference. And the subsequent ad campaign that we did for *Chemical Engineering* won the "Business Marketing Association's Top Award...again, with extensive publicity and a featured spot at their Annual Conference. This exposure put us on the map as a "hot shop" and led to numerous new business opportunities.

Our deliverables campaign also persuaded *Texas Gulf Sulfur* to hire us to create their new corporate image campaign...designed to establish their name change to *TGS* and to support their product line diversification. Again, we created an award winning campaign, this one running in *Business Week*, *Fortune*, and other magazines read by top management.

In addition to *Chemical Engineering* and *Texas Gulf Sulfur*, we signed four other good size accounts as a direct result of our initial hand-made deliverables program. And as our work was seen, more and more doors opened to us. Increasingly, potential clients invited us to participate in their new agency searches. We were on our way up!

❖　❖　❖　❖

The late 1960s was an exciting transitional time in the advertising business. Creativity was in...as bright young boutique shops were making industry giants look dated and boring. Doyle Dane Bernbach's ads made Volkswagen and Levy's Rye Bread top sellers. Ads were fun and memorable and talked about...and most importantly...effective. And we were right there, breaking the old rules in a time called the "Golden Age of Advertising". And to our benefit, we were one of the only agencies bringing this level of creativity to the industrial sector.

So we quickly grew, adding staff and adding space in the form of two upper floor apartments in our building. It became obvious that we'd soon have to move to a larger consolidated space, so our eyes turned to a new building nearing completion at

48th Street and First Avenue. Occupying a full square block, it overlooked the United Nations to the south...the East River to the east...and Beekman Place to the north. Owned by Alcoa, the building featured 7-floors of commercial space, topped by two residential towers. The commercial space had an entrance lobby on 48th Street, and the residential towers had their own separate entrance on 49th Street. Our official address would be 866 United Nations Plaza. Pretty classy!

Being one of the first companies to visit the site even before the interior walls were constructed, we were given our choice of space and location. We picked the fourth floor overlooking the UN and the East River.

❖　❖　❖　❖

But all was not roses! Internal problems were emerging. Bill Fenwick was showing signs of erratic behavior. John and I could sense it, but only realized the extent of the problem when the president of *Standard Gauge* called John to express his company's grave concern. Their company's critical new product launch program was dependent on a massive new catalog that WB&F was creating for them. Not only was the catalog way behind schedule and the pre-production elements full of what they called "inexcusable errors"...they had documentary proof that Bill had been lying to them about things for some weeks. They said they liked Bill, but could no longer trust him. They asked for an immediate change to bail things out.

In a long evening discussion, John and I compared notes and agreed that the problem ran even deeper. Stress or something more severe had changed the Bill we knew. Suffice it to say... as painful as it was for all of us...we had an intervention with Bill and then offered to buy him out. He reluctantly accepted. (Some weeks later, Bill's wife Kay stopped by to thank us. She said she had feared that the stress he was under at the Agency was killing him. But now free of the pressure, he was back to his old amazing self. Soon after, he accepted a great spot on the client side—with Exxon in Houston.)

And then there was some bad news about money! During our first few years in business, we had been adding good accounts, adding great staff, and banking a nice profit. Then, in a single phone call, we learned that all our profits for the past 18-months would be wiped out. One of our major accounts had just announced bankruptcy, with losses so great that we'd be lucky to eventually get pennies on the dollar for all our long-overdue unpaid invoices. It also meant that four of our staffers would have to go.

This would be my first experience in firing anyone. I felt terrible and had a sleepless night before calling in the first of them to break the bad news. It didn't go well. The first was an older guy in our production department, who wore two hearing aids and didn't quite understand my somewhat apologetic ramblings, in an attempt to let him down gently. Suddenly, he got it and yelled out—*"You're firing me?"* Then he pointed out my window to a passing garbage barge on the East River, declaring—*"You see that barge? You're throwing me on it to be dumped into the*

Ocean! You have absolutely no conscience!" All I could say was— *"Sorry"* and hand him his severance check. I felt so bad, that before dinner at home that night I had to take a very long hot shower. And I had three more staffers to go the following day!

But this was the advertising agency business, where turnover is not only to be expected, it's the norm—as agencies adjust their staffs up and down to match client workloads...adding more people when a new account is signed, cutting people when an account is lost. That's why most people in the agency business keep their resumes always out there, and more often than not, a severed employee moves on to an even better spot in just days. I soon learned that. And while it's never easy to fire someone, it's a skill you quickly learn as an agency head.

❖ ❖ ❖ ❖

In the 1960s and 70s, Advertising was considered a very glamorous business. And Ad Agency execs were seen as movers and shakers...admired for their creativity and powers of persuasion...and assumed to be sophisticated in all aspects of the popular culture. If you've ever seen the HBO series—*"Mad Men"*—you've seen exactly what it was like during the first decade or so of our business. The staffers, the clients, the situations, the clothes, even the office furniture...which uncannily was almost identical to our office furniture. And I personally attended some of the industry events portrayed on the show. But Warner, Bicking & Fenwick differed in one important way from *"Mad Men"*. Yes, there was some drinking and lots of smoking... but there was no carousing. Unlike some other agencies, we hardly ever entertained clients, other than at lunch. And if there was any debauchery going on, inside or outside the Agency, I absolutely never saw it or was aware of it. We were all too busy working. And as "good Catholic boys", we tried to set a good example and let everyone know our standards. Even bad language was never tolerated in the Agency...at least in my presence. My ITSM experience had shown me how easily corruption could begin to set in, unless you maintained pretty high standards.

A new Partner—
With Bill Fenwick gone, and now with just two of us as remaining partners, John Bicking worried that if we ever had a major disagreement, there'd be no way to resolve it. So he suggested that we add three outsiders to our board-of-directors...Cliff Chu our attorney, a retired management consultant (can't remember his name), and Phil Gisser...John's old boss at U.S. Industrial Chemicals. At the time, Phil was also President of the Association of Industrial Advertisers, which gave him numerous valuable new business contacts.

All that went well, and when Phil's term as AIA President ended, we invited him to buy-into the agency as a one-third owner. But we kept the name "Warner, Bicking & Fenwick, Inc." because that name was now well established, and because it had a nicely distinctive Anglo-Saxon ring to it.

John thought that Phil 'could walk on water', right up until after he became a full partner. While all three of us pretty much agreed on advertising and marketing strategies for our clients, Phil and John were 180-degree opposites in their views on the best way to manage our business. And the problem worsened over the five years that Phil was with us. Their bitter disputes increasingly put me in the role of being a referee between them. As such, critical decision-making was effectively paralyzed... threatening the Agency's very existence.

Ultimately, I felt I had no alternative but to employ what they'd call today—"The Nuclear Option". I called John and Phil together in the conference room and announced that effective immediately, I was resigning my position in the Agency to start my own shop. I told them that I saw WB&F 'sinking' as a result of our inability to manage the business effectively. And that I had no intention 'of going down with the ship'.

After giving them several minutes to digest my pronouncement, I added—
"While I certainly won't poach any of WB&F's existing accounts... I'd entertain an offer to buy-out your shares in WB&F if the price was right...because obviously, it will be much easier for me to start my new agency with some existing business." And with that, I left the conference room saying—*"Come see me, if you'd like to sell."*

Phil was the first to visit my office. He offered to sell me his one-third interest in WB&F for his original investment price. I agreed, we shook hands and Phil left...soon to become a senior consultant with *Booze, Allen, Hamilton*, where his success flourished. The next day John came to see me, suggesting that with Phil gone...and since we'd always worked well together...he'd like to have us remain a 50-50 partnership under the WB&F banner. I'd become chairman and he'd become president....

swapping our titles and roles. My announced resignation wasn't a ploy to get Phil to sell out. I was serious in my intention to leave them both far behind. But what John suggested made sense and we agreed to leave things as they were...for now.

In hindsight, John and I had complementary roles in the agency... not competing roles. That's why we had no problems working together. I had full say in the creative side of the business...and he had full say in the administrative and financial side of the business. And from the beginning, we had always respected each other's domain. In a sense, we needed each other to succeed. We might debate issues, but almost always "the one in charge" made the final decision.

But as you'll see much later in this memoir, over time John was becoming more and more difficult to deal with. And ultimately, we parted ways...never to speak again.

To his credit, John Bicking was a brilliant and visionary businessman. While initially he was involved in some client work, he increasingly focused his time on the administrative and financial side of the business. He developed WB&F's proprietary computer system, which made the agency more efficient and more profitable. And he set up various tax-advantaged profit-sharing plans that significantly increased our retirement nest eggs. And ultimately, he made the agency an ESOP company (Employee Stock Ownership Plan), which enabled John and I to sell our shares in the agency on very favorable terms.

There were also a few false starts, in John's attempt to diversify the business...attempts that lost us a fair amount of money. We bought and published *"Madison Avenue Magazine"*...a respected trade magazine that had fallen on hard times. We threw in the towel two years later. But at least it showcased WB&F in the form of my monthly column...*"Madison Avenue Merry-go-round"*.

Another venture was our buying into a computer start-up company, headed by our former IBM Account Manager. This had nothing to do with the ad business, but we became a majority partner anyway. That too folded after two years.

Bottom line—for almost 30-years, John and I were partners and co-owners of WB&F and its successor companies. I was responsible for bringing in the money. He was responsible for making sure we kept more of it. For that, I'm most grateful. But ultimately, several key factors grew us apart. (More on that later.)

❖　❖　❖　❖

Clients—

As a full-service agency, we spent considerably more time with each client than is typical for an agency just doing ads and commercials. As such, we had fewer but larger accounts than many agencies our size. It also meant that we were more intimately involved in helping them shape their marketing and competitive strategies. All of which thrust us into unexpectedly close personal relationships with our clients.

When I first saw the broader implications of these close relationships, I told my partners—*"I always thought we had opened this place for one primary reason...to do great creative work for our clients. But I now see that we're actually in two different businesses. The Advertising Agency business...and a second business that should probably be called Hand-Holders, Inc."*

With most of our clients, there seemed to come a time when they wanted you to become their 'personal confidant'. They'd start telling you things that they didn't feel comfortable telling their bosses, co-workers, subordinates, and sometimes even their spouses. They'd see you as a safe and informed ally ...who not only knew their company and its cast-of-characters...but who had the broader experience to advise them wisely. Again and again, you'd hear them say—*"I'd like you to become part of my personal support group!"* You'd have little alternative but to say, "yes"... even though you might prefer to have a more distant and strictly professional relationship.

Obviously, all this adds to the time you have to spend with the client. But, as I'd learn, it was a very important element in holding and growing an account. And there were other non-business rewards...many of the clients seeking this kind of close relationship were very fine, highly ethical, fun-to-be-with business people. And helping them personally was somewhat of a privilege, as it might be with any good friend. But alas, there were more than a few clients that I would have preferred to keep at a distance. I minimized personal contact with these as best I could. And when that was not possible, I'd often resign their account.

In most firms, the principals spend most of their day managing the overall business. In a small agency, the principals necessarily spend almost all of their day directly involved in client work. That means that all of the administrative tasks have to be handled after hours and on weekends. During our first year or so, I rarely got home before 10:00PM, as we hand-tabulated employee timesheets into specific invoice billing codes (e.g.- copywriting, photo supervision, printing supervision, editorial contact, etc.) and applied the appropriate hourly rates...for each of the many dozens of individual projects being worked upon. Since everything...including work-in-progress... was billed monthly, the administrative workload in this age before computers was significant. And as a fee-based business, invoice accuracy was essential, both for speedy client approval and prompt payment. That's why in the early days, we didn't delegate billing preparation to a clerical employee...even if we could afford one.

As our business grew, we knew that these 'back office' tasks would prove overwhelming. So John Bicking set us on the road to computerization. Back then, the technology was limited to punch cards and mechanical sorters. There were no word processors. Our invoices had to be compiled and typed by hand. But then IBM introduced their first mini-computer. And WB&F became the first ad agency in New York to fully computerize. In fact, IBM used us as the demo site to showcase their system, bringing the CFOs and COOs of several major agencies to our offices. I guess that made us a leading-edge shop. And Phil Doherty in his *NY Times* ad column called us exactly that!

❖   ❖   ❖   ❖

The Good. The Bad. And the Ugly—

I loved the advertising business. And my career at Warner, Bicking & Fenwick was an overall joy, even though the hours were crazy...with an 83-hour work week, plus a 90-minute commute both mornings and evenings. But as time went on, more and more of these work hours were spent outside of the office... either at client locations or at home. After dinner, I'd often work upstairs in my study until the wee hours, including at least one day on most weekends.

Despite those enormous time demands, I still enjoyed it all... because it was always new, and never repetitious. We faced a new creative challenge almost every week, giving us yet another opportunity to come up with a unique solution. As a kid, I loved making things. And the agency business let me make lots of things...and actually get paid for it.

Over the many years that we were in business, I got to work with more than a hundred great companies...intimately involved in their marketing plans and growth strategies...and contributing in important ways that were usually gratefully received. There were exceptions of course. Some clients proved difficult to deal with...being abusive, or exploitive, or unprofitable...or all three. Is short, they were just not a good fit. These we resigned, trying to replace them with clients better suited to our strengths. And admittedly, a few times we were fired for screw-ups on our part. And several clients left us due to mergers and reorganizations within their corporations. But all in all, our client turnover was about typical for the industry.

Our work not only won us new clients and broad industry recognition...it won us more than 100 creative awards...including a CLIO. Our coverage in the *NY Times* and *Advertising Age* was extensive. And I was invited to be a guest speaker or panelist at dozens of ad industry conferences. All this was an important part of increasing our visibility and our exposure to potential new clients. I also spoke at and ran sessions at most of our clients' sales meetings, usually held at great resorts around the U.S. and in the Caribbean...all part of servicing our accounts and cementing the relationships.

When we started the agency, 90-percent of our clients were within walking distance of our offices. At the 10 year point, 90-percent were in the suburbs or a plane ride away. In those early days, we handled mainly industrial accounts. Over time, we expanded into hi-tech and business service accounts...then into high-ticket consumer products like cameras and stereo equipment. And toward the end of my time at the agency, we had a major division serving food product accounts.

One factor that worked to our great advantage over the years was our reputation in helping foreign companies enter and succeed in the U.S. market. This reputation was enhanced by our location right next to the United Nations, close to all the foreign embassies and delegations. During my time at the Agency, we had major clients with headquarters in Germany, Switzerland, Italy, England, Japan, and Canada.

All that was the "Good".

The "Bad" were those accounts we ultimately resigned because they didn't meet our informal corporate goal of…"having fun and making money". One without the other was OK. But if both were lacking, we knew it was time to move on.

The "Ugly" were those few accounts who tortured or cheated us. In all cases, it was not the company itself…it was the specific executive or executives we had to deal with. Thankfully, our business was good enough that we didn't have to put up with them for too long. Again, the vital importance of an ongoing new business effort…because clients come and go!

(You'll find a list of some of our major clients in the Addenda section.)

❖   ❖   ❖   ❖

February 1969—On the home front—
After seven years of living in our cozy house in Washington Township, we finally made the move to a far bigger place in Ridgewood, NJ.

Anne had found us a wonderful 12-room English Manor-style home. Built in 1919, it had all the charm and space we had hoped for. The move was long overdue. Our old house had no family room, no dining room, and no garage. With a family of five (Chris wouldn't be born until 3-years later) we were definitely squeezed in…even though we had added a second-story dormer with a third bedroom, a small bath, and home office.

The Washington Township home had cost us $17,000 back in 1961. The dormer expansion added another $4,000 to our investment...kept that low only because we did much of the work ourselves. And when we finally sold it for $47,000 in 1969, we netted a nice profit, even after paying off our mortgage.

We purchased the new Ridgewood house for $65,000...which frankly we could only afford to buy and furnish thanks to the inheritance that Anne had received from her deceased Uncle Ronald's estate. Thanks to her, we at last had a beautiful home with lots of room, in a lovely town with great schools and lots of amenities. And we would remain happily there for 45 years until 2014.

❖   ❖   ❖   ❖

Warner, Bicking & Fenwick, Inc.
—Course Correction—

October 1970—My third Mentor—

After six years in business, WB&F was doing well...adding clients and staff and enjoying a great reputation. It was full speed ahead with only an occasional blip. But then, a single phone call brought me into contact with Mentor #3...and that set me on a new course that I would never have embarked upon without him.

His name was Charles Ramsey...better known as "Ram"...and he was president of an association of independent ad agencies called TAAN (the "Transamerican Advertising Agency Network"). Ram was in New York to select a new TAAN member, and we agreed to meet that afternoon to learn more about each other. I had never heard of TAAN, but Ram sounded like such a delightful guy that I cleared my afternoon schedule. Little did I know that this phone call and meeting would change my life so profoundly for the better. Ram would become a true Mentor and friend, opening my eyes to a whole world of concepts and opportunities.

Basically, TAAN was an informal group of mid-size, privately owned, non-competing ad agencies in key markets around the country...plus an agency in Canada and one in Japan. (It would later expand to add more than a dozen agencies around the world to become the "Transworld Advertising Agency Network".) Ram was the retired president of the San Diego member.

In meetings twice a year, TAAN agency owners would openly and candidly share their positive and negative experiences in managing their businesses...along with presenting client case histories and detailing their latest new business techniques. And TAAN would bring in expert guest speakers. All this sounded great. Sort of an MBA in running a successful ad agency. In addition, as a member of the TAAN Network, we could also provide branch office services to each other, should the need for local assistance arise. This feature alone would help us more effectively compete with large multi-office agencies in a new business pitch. Hearing all this, we decided to sign on, and John Bicking suggested that I be the WB&F person to attend all the TAAN meetings.

My first TAAN meeting was in Key Biscayne, Florida. At age 34, I was probably the youngest member at the meeting. But as Ram told me they would, everyone in the group welcomed me as an old friend and full partner. I was impressed by the quality of their ideas and their candor. And I thought to myself how lucky I'd be to have any one of these guys as a business partner. (Yes, they were all men, but a few years later, we'd have some female agency owners in the group.) As a key part of every meeting, there were informal, small group, problem-solving sessions. Two of the sessions that I attended at my first meeting really stood out—

The owner of our San Francisco TAAN agency described how the new VP of Marketing at one of his largest accounts had just put the pressure on him for what amounted to a monthly cash 'kick back'. Of course, the agency would never do this, because it was both unethical and illegal. And the agency would, of course, have to report this situation to the client's upper management. The problem was how to handle it without the likely 'he-said/

he-said' counter claims resulting in the agency being terminated along with the dishonest VP. I listened with amazement as a few members offered some very practical and effective strategies, based on their own experiences with dishonest clients. Wow!

Another TAAN member described a partner problem. He had become convinced that his partner...a 51-percent owner...was psychotic. Getting him out without sinking the business was the challenge. Again, the shared experiences and suggestions were amazing.

But one thing troubled me—all their talk about management succession and early retirement. I loved the business and with a six-year-old agency saw myself as only just getting started. Getting out early was never even a remote thought or option, so I asked Ram why everyone seemed so preoccupied with planning for their retirement. That's when Ram laid out his views—that planning for a 'second career' was by far the most important challenge an agency owner faced. I asked him to expand on this whole concept and tell me precisely how it all worked. In the long one-on-one session that followed, his logic was so eye opening and persuasive that I decided then and there that I would change my focus in managing the business...so that I could realistically leave to start a 'second career' at age 50 or so.

Ram pointed out that the Ad Agency Business was basically a young person's business...not unlike sports or pop music. While a total joy full of accolades at the outset, there'd eventually come a time where your staff and your clients would be younger than your kids. A time when you'd start to hate the music in your own commercials. A time when you'd likely start repeating yourself in your creative work...and as a result, see your business decline. Or find yourself shoved aside by young staffers who viewed you as the past, not the future. Far better to get out when you "still have your legs" and your reputation. But to get out...not to some boring retirement...but rather to a richly fulfilling 'second career', specifically crafted to excite you. That's the secret to not growing old! The secret that lets you...at mid-life...rejuvenate both your mind and your spirit...with exciting new challenges and satisfactions. In the fullest sense, this is a strategy that lets you live two fulfilling lives in one! But it becomes feasible, only if you begin planning for it well in advance.

Per Ram, the most important decision an agency owner can make...after that initial decision to start the business...is deciding when to get out. Pick your future target date...discuss it with your spouse...write it down and put that note in the safe deposit box...and then draw up a detailed plan on how to make it become achievable. You'll need that plan to come away from the business with enough money to live on for the rest of your life...and to subsidize your second career, which you'll no doubt embark on more for its sheer pleasure than its income. And equally important, you'll need a plan to lay the groundwork for your second career, long before you depart the agency...so that you are ready to launch right after a well-deserved short vacation with family and maybe a few friends.

He said that in your dreams, you probably envision that selling your agency is...you being honored at a Testimonial Dinner and receiving a big bag of gold. But it almost never happens that way. You may get the dinner, but most all the money you'll receive will be based on the agency's future success after you've gone. And unless you've recruited and empowered outstanding succession management, the agency might falter without you. And even with good management and a rock solid compensation agreement, you can't be certain about the size of your "pay out", because clients and key staffers can quickly depart. In the agency business...unlike many other businesses...there are no tangible assets to sell, nothing really there to secure your future income.

That means your plan requires creating your own "early retirement nest egg". And thanks to the power of compound interest, that's quite doable if you start the process early enough. A good rule-of-thumb is investing at least 20-percent of your personal income each year into your "nest egg" fund. And that means resisting the temptation to underpay yourself, so that you can plow everything back into the agency's growth. The business may prosper, but in the long-term you won't. As one senior TAAN member advised—"*A dollar not taken today, is a dollar lost forever!*"

Of equal importance to implementing an aggressive financial plan, is your informed selection of a 'second career'...and your advanced preparations for it. While running his San Diego agency, Ram bought a property in Montana and began developing it into what became *The Buffalo Jump Ranch*...a working ranch that he operated after leaving his agency at age 50. Another member along with his wife formed a high-level consulting firm affiliated with the *American Management Association*, conducting small group seminars for the CEOs of major corporations around the world. Yet another became a successful novelist and film writer. And another, a well-known artist with his own gallery. Even my own business partner, John Bicking, later started a 'second career'. Along with his wife Marilyn, they opened a raptor rehabilitation center in Moab, Utah...fully licensed to treat injured eagles, hawks, and other endangered raptors. All these 'second career' choices brought them particular joy...and invigorated their lives at a time when boredom might otherwise have begun to set in. None of them were embarked on for the money. All of them were embarked on at the peak of the TAAN Member's talents and energy!

But obviously, it took considerable advanced planning to successfully embark on any of these 'second careers'. In most cases several years, in laying the groundwork and perfecting the skills to hit the ground running "after they quit their day jobs." But that was the fun of it...a refreshing diversion from the daily demands of always prioritizing client and staff problems! Bottom line—make yourself your own most important client... and use all your expertise to develop a detailed plan for your own post-agency success!

This whole concept of a 'second career' was tremendously appealing to me, because there were so many things I hoped to do in my lifetime...but things that I realized my very demanding advertising agency career might never permit. So I set my target 'exit date' for June 1987...almost 16 years away. Obviously, a lot could happen in those intervening years. And quite possibly my choice for my 'second career' might change. In which case, I could always modify or restructure my plan. Even so, there was absolutely no downside, because creating a sizeable "nest egg" while still fairly young, would give me far far more future options.

❖   ❖   ❖   ❖

Over the years I learned a tremendous amount from the other TAAN members. Some became role models, and a few became negative role models...providing up-close examples of how easy it is to screw-up one's life and career through booze, carousing, and believing your own press releases. But no one gave me as many practical business-life insights as Ram. The importance of managing your career, and not just your agency. Not taking yourself too seriously. Not 'falling in love' with your clients or staffers...recognizing that one day they'll probably all abandon you. Not compromising in work or in life. And above all, having fun and keeping perspective in the business.

Here's just one example of Ram's wisdom and its powerful influence on me and our family. Up until TAAN, I had always put the agency first, rarely ever taking a vacation. Family plans always took a back seat to client needs. I can't even remember how many times I cancelled personal travel plans, or cut short a trip to the shore. Recognizing that we all had a tendency to do this, Ram made attendance at our twice-yearly TAAN meetings compulsory and encouraged members to bring along their families to at least one meeting a year. This gave me a business rationale (and a legitimate client excuse) to take one or even two family vacations a year. And most importantly...by being there, it gave Anne and the kids a vastly greater understanding of "The Warner Family Business" and all it entailed...the crazy hours, the demanding clients, the sometimes wacky people...so unlike the 9-to-5 corporate families in our New Jersey neighborhood. And because TAAN meetings were most often held in member locations, we got to vacation in some truly wonderful places around the U.S. and around the World. It's hard not to be extremely grateful to the guy who had done that for you and your family!

❖ ❖ ❖ ❖

What was Ram like? And why did so many of us value his counsel and his friendship? Ram was what you'd call a 'guy's-guy'. As down-to-earth as a guy could possibly be. A fantastic storyteller. Funny, but deadly serious when offering his advice or opinion... often followed by a hearty laugh, as if to say—*"you can ignore all this if you want."* Smart as hell. A born leader, more than likely honed during his time as an Army Captain during World War II. While prep school educated in the North East, he made his home out West. Though he still bought his dress-up clothes at Brooks Brothers, he wore western shirts and Levi pants and jackets more often than not. Though he lived in stylish La Jolla, he was an avid outdoorsman...an expert hunter and serious fly-fisherman. Big Game trophies in his home and office were testimony to his skills.

The more you got to know Ram, the more your realized his near celebrity status in San Diego and even parts of Montana and Mexico. He served on several influential civic and business boards and was pals with friends ranging from retired Admirals, to politicians, to restaurant owners, to corporate CEOs, to neighborhood characters. And a few times a year, he'd lead a small group of friends on hunting trips in Mexico or Alaska.

When I first met him, Ram was 56...22 years my senior. So I guess that could have made him something of a father figure. But that's not right. He was more like a slightly older brother, looking out for me. But more than that—he was a true Mentor and friend, in the very fullest sense...opening my eyes to all those new possibilities.

What did he look like? About 6-foot tall, slim, muscular, unpretentious. But his bushy moustache, high forehead, and twinkling eyes suggested that he was no ordinary guy. And indeed, he was no ordinary guy! He was truly one of a kind!

(Ram died in Montana on February 25, 2001 at age 87...just two-months after the death of his beloved wife Lieth. He influenced so many of us that soon after, 30 of us got together to publish a book called—"*Remembering Ram...The wisdom and wit of Charles C. Ramsey, recalled by those he mentored and befriended.*" He blessed all our lives!)

❖   ❖   ❖   ❖

When I returned back home after that first TAAN meeting, I filled in John about the 'second career' concept and the necessary implementation strategies that went with it. He was more than enthused, because it fit in perfectly with his own aspirations. John was a great amateur photographer, with Ansel Adams' work as his inspiration. He and Marilyn took most all their vacations in and around the National Parks, where they spent their days photographing the rugged landscapes. They so loved the area that they planned to eventually buy land in Utah. And Marilyn...though still working fulltime as an Operating Room nurse...was a volunteer at a local wildlife center. Her passion there? Caring for raptors...the hawks, eagles, and falcons. So a 'second career' involving both their loves truly excited them.

Anne too, embraced the idea and the start date. She knew that the agency's time demands on me were unsustainable. And that my proposed 'second career' would give us far more time together at the point when our children were leaving home.

To get things rolling, John brought in a top financial planning firm to help us design a series of 'deferred-income' programs that would help us build our personal "nest eggs". Following their advice, we set-up a series of Profit Sharing programs, funded 100-percent by the Agency. While these programs benefited all of our vested employees, they benefitted John and me to a far greater extent than if we had merely increased our salaries and bonuses...both of which would have been taxable. In contrast, all the funds in the programs would grow on a 'tax-deferred' basis...benefitting from compound interest...until we left the Agency and rolled them over into a personal IRA (Individual Retirement Account). Over the ensuing years, John carefully administered the plans, and through wise investments increased our personal 'nest eggs' significantly.

And my own 'second career" plans? The restoration of historic buildings...both homes and commercial properties. I saw that wonderful old buildings could be bought for next to nothing at that time. And with imaginative and sensitive renovation, they could be brought back to their full glory.

I loved touring historic properties and building sites...and loved all aspects of the building trades...from conceptual design through final construction. I had built an extensive library on these topics. And gained hands-on experience in extensively renovating our Ridgewood home. In addition, I had earned my "Certificate in Historic Preservation" from Montclair State University.

But as noted before, things can change pretty dramatically over time. My interest in historic restoration never waned. But the economics definitely did. The debut of "This Old House" on PBS seven-years later, prompted a rush to buy up historic properties at premium prices. Add the cost of quality restoration, and the potential was no longer attractive. But happily, I had an even more appealing back-up plan for my 'second career'...succeeding Ram as TAAN president. More on that later.

❖   ❖   ❖   ❖

August 1974—My fourth Mentor—

Anne and I had made many close friends in TAAN. And as mentioned, I learned a tremendous amount from them. But it was an unplanned event with the member I admired most that set my agency on a new strategic course that made the rest of my advertising career more profitable, more productive, and far more satisfying.

That TAAN member was Bill Boylhart, who headed his own very successful ad agency in Los Angeles. Even though Bill and his wife Lynn were almost 15-years older than Anne and I, we had so many mutual interests that we really enjoyed spending time together during and after our TAAN meetings. And that's what brought all four of us together in Nantucket following our TAAN meeting in Maine.

Relaxing and chatting in Nantucket's 'Club Car' bar, I casually asked Bill why he decided to go into advertising and start his own agency. His answer stunned me. With a smile he said— *"To make lots of money."* If asked, my own answer would have been—*"To have the personal freedom to do my best work."* The money aspects were really never part of my motivation. Certainly, I hoped to make a comfortable income. But that took a back seat to achieving creative independence.

I knew Bill's agency did great work and had a stellar reputation that he was extremely proud of. So I knew there was much more behind his perhaps-joking answer. So I asked him to elaborate. And that's when he shared his "Managing for Profits" concept and its well-crafted strategy. As Bill laid it all out for me, I had another one of those 'Eureka Moments'. And it was then and there that Bill truly became my fourth Mentor!

As Bill explained it—Every company wants both growth and profits, but almost always they sacrifice profits for growth... with 20-percent of their customers, or clients, actually providing most all of their profits...while the remaining 80-percent are at breakeven or worse. The company will often tout their growing size as an indicator of their strength...but underneath, their financial state can be fragile. Maybe that's OK for a hi-tech start-up seeking investors betting on the future, but it's not the best way to run a successful privately-owned company.

If your goal is "Managing for Profits", you make and adhere to a number of key strategic decisions, all based on their profit potential. These include—1. The market segments and types of clients that you target. 2. The specific products and services that you offer. 3. The staff needed to succeed. 4. The compensation system that fully rewards all your efforts.

Quite simply, in our chosen field of advertising—<u>You build an agency that can uniquely provide superior services and results for those companies that offer you the greatest profit potential.</u>

And guess what? You'll no doubt find that these are the types of clients where you can do your best work. They'll expect it, and appreciate it, and will reward you for it. And if that's not always the case—"Managing for Profits" gives you the financial strength to resign that account and move on to another client who will properly reward your best efforts. Knowing all this, adds even more to the personal satisfaction that we all hope for in this business.

❖ ❖ ❖ ❖

Wow! I got it! And this was not just some textbook theory. It was
proven in practice at Bill's very successful Los Angeles ad agency.
So almost immediately after returning home to New York, we
began to redirect WB&F's strategy to "Managing for Profits".

Before the transformation, we had 26 clients and a staff of 56.
Three years later, we had a far more carefully chosen group of
clients...a maximum of 10, by design. And though our total payroll costs remained pretty much unchanged, we now had a far
smaller, but far more experienced staff of just 28. Our services
were expanded to include marketing consulting, new product
development, test marketing, and dealer support programs...
along with an expanded market research division. As a result,
our total billings more than doubled, and our profits more than
quadrupled. And WB&F's reputation for being more than just
an ad agency became well established. Further, we were able to
assemble an impressive number of client case histories that set
us apart in our new business presentations.

Core to our "Managing for Profits" plan was our strategic decision to specialize in serving a certain type of client. We specifically targeted AAA-rated clients that had a large sales force and/
or dealer network. Clients that introduced their new integrated
advertising and sales support programs annually... at large sales
meetings or at major trade shows. Ideally, they were number-
two or number-three in their fields...and needed a "Big Idea"
to help them gain market share over their far-larger-spending
competitors. Ideally, they also had new products to introduce,

213

where test marketing could help them determine the optimum pricing, competitive positioning, and demand potential at different ad spending levels.

To deliver results for clients like these, we needed the best and most experienced people we could find. No more juniors or entry-level people. Staffers who could hit the ground running... without need for middle-management supervisors, because they could get it right the very first time.

And since we'd be delivering expanded and more costly services to each client, we needed a way to help them manage their overall spending through us. So we developed a proprietary budget management system that tracked and forecast costs for each of the dozens of projects planned for the year. This removed their, and our, worry that overall spending might be out-of-control and exceed their annual budget. This was particularly important with our fee-based compensation system...where we billed for actual hours expended, rather than on a fixed-bid project basis.

Without doubt, Bill Boylhart's "Managing for Profits" strategy proved an important key to WB&F's financial success. But more than that, it let us have far closer relationships with client top management. And it kept me personally invigorated... learning new skills so that I could contribute more and more to our clients' overall business success.

❖   ❖   ❖   ❖

Anne and my relationship with the Boylharts continued throughout their lifetimes. They hosted us at their California waterfront home in Newport Beach...just across the street from John Wayne's place...and at their summer home in Orient Point, at the tip of Long Island's north fork. And after we had our Nantucket home, they visited us there several times. Then after Lynn's passing, Bill would spend a week or so with us in Nantucket each year, until age and illness finally made his travels no longer possible. Bill shared so much with me...and I'm so pleased that in his later years, I could help him when he sought my advise on a number of personal matters. It was always a lively give-and-take between we two close friends!

Bill Boylhart was far more than a brilliant businessman. And his early life was pretty amazing. When America entered World War II, Bill volunteered to become an Army pilot. As a teenager, he had flown stunt planes in local Air Shows and was already an expert aviator. The Army quickly signed him up and sent him off to Officer Candidate School. But while there, he learned that the Army currently had far more pilots than airplanes... so they put him through Anti-Aircraft training...explaining that he could shoot down enemy planes to even up the score. While there, one of the trainers told him that just before receiving your commission, the Army would ask your preferred assignment location. And nine-times-out-of-ten they'd give you the exact opposite. So Bill asked to be assigned to an anti-aircraft station in Alaska...and predictably, they gave him a post in Hollywood instead!

Well it seems that about 6-months after Bill's arrival in Holly-wood, the resident British Film Community decided to organize a big party... *"To thank American servicemen for their gallant support of England in its time of direst need."* And Greer Garson... the famous British actress and the group's president...wrote to the Commanding General in the area to request help in providing the refreshments, this being a time of strict food rationing. After his OK, the General bumped the request down his chain of command...until it finally landed on Lt. Bill Boylhart's desk. It got there because Bill's superior didn't like Bill at all, and hoped he'd screw things up. (Apparently Bill had consistently scored higher than his boss in both artillery practice and readiness aptitude tests.)

To his boss's total annoyance, the event proved to be a huge success. And in her 'thank you' letter to the General, Greer Garson specifically singled out Lt. Bill Boylhart for his invaluable help. Per standard military procedures, a copy of that letter was inserted into Bill's service file.

We now move to Salerno, Italy...where American Forces under General Mark Clark had just begun their assault to free Europe from the Nazis. And Bill's artillery unit was part of the landing contingent. They say an Army runs on its stomach. And that certainly proved to be the case when General Clark ordered that his mess officer be replaced...because the General found his bread to be inedible. Someone quickly dug into the files... and that Greer Garson letter in praise of Lt. Boylhart stood out. So Bill was immediately pulled from his artillery unit and re-assigned to be General Clark's new mess officer.

Bill quickly assessed the problem. The bakers were all young German POWs, trained to make their bread with one-part flour and two-parts sawdust. They insisted that this was the only way to make good bread, because their superiors had told them so. Though the Americans had plenty of flour, the bakers refused to use it to replace the sawdust. So rather than argue with them in his faulty German or find new bakers, Bill simply had all the sawdust carted away, saying it was desperately needed elsewhere. The bakers were then forced against their better judgment to use the "inferior" all-flour bread recipe that Bill gave them. And he didn't stop there. Commandeering a truck and a few servicemen, he 'requisitioned" meat, vegetables, and food supplies from all of the invasion force unloading areas... declaring it—"For the personal mess of General Mark Clark." And he bartered with some locals for fresh dairy and seafood.

The General was happy, and Bill survived as General Clark's mess officer. But he might not have survived if Greer Garson had never written that letter. You see, while Bill was still supervising the General's kitchen, his artillery unit was deployed north to be part of the horrific Monte Casinno assault...where most of them were killed in months of fighting. Bill was only sent north, two months after Monte Casinno had been taken.

I only learned this story some years after Bill and I had become friends...as we shared details of our somewhat unusual military experiences. His was certainly more exciting than mine! He dodged Generals and then bullets, while I effectively dodged only the draft!

217

Bill's interests beyond advertising were extensive. He was an expert sailor...with a classic 37-foot wood-hulled Egg Harbor cruiser once owned by the actress Deanna Durbin. He was an acknowledged scrimshaw expert...with the largest and finest collection in private hands. He built museum-quality model ships...full-rigged clipper ships and historic men-of–war. He did beautiful bird woodcarvings, published reproductions of early whaling ship logs, and much more. And Lynn did beautiful and unique needlepoint art that was displayed in several galleries and in some private collections. Plus she was an expert in rare botanicals...licensed by the U.S. Department of Agriculture to collect seeds and cuttings from most anywhere in the world. These were all hobbies that Bill and Lynn shared with us over the years.

Of course, I learned far more about running a business from Bill than just "Managing for Profits". How he sold his agency, and the fall-out, was particularly instructive. It seems that he received a call one day from the CEO of 'Doremus & Company'... a very large ad and public relations agency headquartered in New York City. Doremus had been trying, with only modest success, to secure a position in the West Coast market. And they approached Bill with the thought of a possible alliance or merger. At the time, Bill not only headed his own very successful agency, but was also president and chairman of the 72-member "Western States Advertising Agencies Association". Intrigued by the opportunity, Bill agreed to a meeting...preparing for it with intensive research on both Doremus and the opportunities open to them in California and the surrounding States. In the fullest sense, he developed a marketing plan for Doremus, just as if they had been one of his clients.

They were so impressed that they asked Bill if he would ever consider not just a merger, but becoming their top guy in the West...heading up all the Doremus operations in Los Angeles, San Francisco, Portland, Seattle, and Phoenix, for starters. Bill told them he would give it serious consideration and discuss it with his partners. They agreed to meet again the following week at Doremus Headquarters in New York.

After an Agency tour and meeting all the Doremus key players, Bill gave them a sheet with a list of his 14 requirements, should he accept their proposal. Compensation, benefits, stock purchase price, employment agreement details, an appointment to the Doremus board of directors, etc. were all included...along with two special requirements—1. That Bill's agency remain a member of TAAN. 2. That all his agency's employees have job security for at least two years (unless guilty of misconduct). He added that most of these things he already enjoyed or controlled as his agency's principal owner, and as such had no incentive to lose them.

Somewhat startled over Bill's preparation and his bold initiative, the Doremus officers carefully reviewed Bill's requirements and ultimately agreed to them all...with the exception of the employee security issue. They found this unprecedented and said it could cause a problem with their current staff, few of whom had employment agreements. But Bill felt so strongly about it that he offered to reduce his stock sale price if they agreed to it. The deal was struck and Bill became a Doremus officer and Board Member. His contract was for five years, and his bonus was based on increased agency <u>income</u>...not profits.

(Doremus wanted to grow, regardless of costs...with the goal of being acquired by a publicly traded giant agency conglomerate. In this they succeeded, soon becoming an Omnicom Company.) The Doremus Chairman later confided to Bill that the board was initially put off by the size and scope of Bill's requirements. But then they concluded that an executive this organized and decisive was exactly what they needed!

All went according to plan, with one major downside. Upon learning of the merger, two disgruntled employees started loudly proclaiming that Bill had sold them all out for his personal gain. This infected many on his staff, who turned on him with nasty comments and letters and more. His attempt to protect them was disbelieved and ignored. Bill certainly did very well financially, but any hope of being remembered fondly by his staff was dashed to smithereens. I could tell that this affected him strongly. That those he cared for and nurtured would now call him a traitor nearly broke his heart!

The lessons I took away from all this? In buying or selling a business, be the first to firmly state your terms. That lets you negotiate from strength. And don't expect your employees to continue to love you, or even hold you in high regard. Change for many of them will be traumatic, and their emotions will hold sway. They'll see your gain as their loss. Envy will trigger resentment and then anger. And anything special you do for them will be only viewed as guilt...insufficient guilt. So live with it! That's the price the Captain pays when he 'abandons ship'.

Reading all this, you probably picture Bill as a big commanding guy, with a leader's dynamic style. But he was a slight man of only average height. Soft-spoken, kindly, and serious, with a gentle laugh. While extremely bright, he was a careful listener, who respected your thoughts and views. But he was always firm in offering his own analysis and recommendations. A man of wide interests and expertise. A great friend. A mentor that I was truly blessed to have.

❖   ❖   ❖   ❖

Not all fun and games—
I've possibly given you the impression that my advertising career was pretty-much smooth sailing…lots of good times without too many trials and tribulations. So I should probably take a few minutes here to set the record straight. While I loved the business and found it enormously fulfilling, it was a tough business that could chew you up…if you let it.

In the movies back in my day, the ad business was always portrayed as an ulcer-producing occupation. And with good reason. The never-ending client demands, the cutthroat competition, the constant pressure to create award-winning work time after time…while juggling internal disputes between prima-donna staffers. All that could keep you in a state of unrelenting stress.

We had all these pressures and more at WB&F. But thankfully, they never did me in. Probably because of a few 'self-preservation' techniques I used to minimize their impact. Here are a few of them that you might find useful—

Perspective—Even in the darkest of hours, I'd tell myself that there was no need to panic or get despondent. The worse that could happen is that the agency goes under...and that I'd 'live to fight another day'. I could always start over by opening a new shop...or take a senior position at an agency giant who'd probably pay me big bucks. And importantly—I had that sizeable nest-egg set aside to keep me and my family safe and secure for as long as it takes. Reminding yourself of all this, gives you a clear head to deal effectively with the challenges at hand!

But one warning—based on things I've seen at TAAN. Never risk your personal assets to bail out your agency...either with cash or a business loan. In a small business with few physical assets, lenders will almost always insist that you personally secure their loan...putting your house, savings and more at risk. So if your agency goes down, you go down too!

Skipping a few paychecks or making a small personal bridge-loan is fine. But don't sign away your financial security! Better to let the place go under!

Prioritize—With dozens of calls for your attention swirling around in your brain, it's hard to fully concentrate on just one. The others keep popping up as reminders and distractions. Obviously, the answer is to prioritize and laser-focus on just one issue at a time. But that's easier said than done. So I developed a mental exercise that works for me.

In my mind, I envision one of those big Chinese cabinets with fifty or more little drawers. I put each one of my many challenges or calls for attention into its own separate drawer...not to be opened until I'm ready to deal with it. I know that they're all there, safely contained. So I no longer have any concerns that they'll be lost or forgotten. The cabinet gives me the discipline of effectively prioritizing. A discipline that I might otherwise not have!

Multi-Tasking—In running a busy ad agency, you're required to 'wear many hats'—shifting almost seamlessly from artist to accountant...from confidant to enforcer...from marketing guru to humble servant...and more. But those personality shifts are tough to accomplish in their purest forms. For example—Let's say you're working quietly in your office, trying to perfect a proposal for a new client...when suddenly someone barges through your closed door with a major staff crisis. It's hard not to be annoyed at the interruption, and that annoyance will certainly affect your attitude as you try to tackle the staff crisis. And once that staff crisis is fully contained, your residual agitation will make it hard to get back to writing that client proposal. Your ability to concentrate and your writing style will both be affected. That's the downside of standard "multi-tasking". Each task suffers a bit from the residual "noise". And frankly, the satisfaction that should go with a job perfectly done is diminished by transitional annoyance.

So how do you eliminate the problem? By harnessing a sort of controlled "multiple personality disorder" that I call "Multi-Living". Sounds a little weird? Maybe. But just consider—

Inside each of us, there actually "live" hundreds of different personalities...some who enjoy solitude...some who enjoy partying...some who love physical challenges...some who enjoy organizing things...some who like combat...etc. (That's why most of us can at times enjoy different kinds of movies—romances, action thrillers, comedies, tear jerkers, dramas, mysteries, etc.) The trick is delegating the specific task at hand to the "inner personality" most qualified to handle that task. That assures not only a job well done...but the greatest level of personal satisfaction while performing that task.

For example, let's go back to that situation where you're thoughtfully writing that client proposal. Someone barges into your office with a staff crisis. Rather than getting annoyed at the interruption...you delegate the task of quelling the crisis to your inner personality best able to quickly resolve it. Be that your inner "Clint Eastwood" or "Mister Rogers" or "Judge Judy" or one of dozens of other personalities that you have somewhere in there. They get the job done, and feel really good about their achievement.

While that's going on, your plan-writing-self takes a well-deserved 'rest break' before resuming the writing task. Everyone's happy. A little whacky? Perhaps. But "Multi-Living" works for me. It <u>maximizes</u> the pleasure found in even the most annoying tasks...and <u>minimizes</u> the annoying distractions that intrude on the things you most enjoy!

This concept works in areas well beyond business. In daily life, some activities are pleasurable, while others are not. Yet we have to do both, whether at work or at home. And in truth, a large part of what makes a required task un-pleasurable is that we're constantly thinking of things we'd rather be doing. So why not delegate that un-pleasurable task to the inner personality who finds that task pleasurable?

A fun little example—After watching a few episodes of the period drama series "Downton Abbey", Anne and I joked that what we really needed was a professional staff like they have at the Abbey—a butler, valet, ladies maid, housekeeper, cook, chauffer, groundsman, etc. They could take over all the many little tasks that we were doing, and take great pride in their jobs well done. Then Anne laughed and said—*"We already have a staff. And they're all us."*

So as a lark, we actually created on paper our own "Household Staff". Then back home, on a little magnetic plaque, we posted this on the side of our refrigerator—

Anne's Staff—Secretary- Julia / Housekeeper- Edith /
      Laundress- Mary / Maid- Annette.
Jack's Staff— Chef- Jacques / Butler- Jeffry / Handyman- Tony /
      Chauffer- Carl.

All were at our disposal and could be relied on to take over their assigned duties brilliantly without hesitation or distraction.

Anne would laughingly say—*"Would you have Jacques serve dinner earlier tonight?"* Or—*"Could you ask Tony to fix that leaking faucet?"* We'd then both laugh, because it turned our routine tasks into a little fun. Also, I found I took more enjoyment in fixing dinner that night or getting out the old toolbox. Self-delusion can be fun!

The gag didn't go on for too long, but it did make our routine tasks a bit more enjoyable. But I include it here because it does illustrate the concept behind what I call "Multi-Living".

❖ ❖ ❖ ❖

REFLECTIONS
—After 15 years of running WB&F—

We started the agency to do great work for our clients, in a field that we loved. And in that, we succeeded beyond our expectations. We had won many awards and achieved an excellent reputation for creativity and innovation. Our client list had expanded from the strictly industrial to business products and services...and we were now adding some high-end consumer product accounts.

By opening our own agency, we had the freedom to be our own bosses...shaping the agency as we saw fit. And the rewards of having your own business were many—not the least of which were the perks.

But running a business was highly demanding. The very long hours. The responsibilities. The never-ceasing requirements for your dedicated attention. And none of us had any experience in running a business before. It was all on-the-job learning...but with the good fortune of having great advice from our TAAN colleagues who had "trod these paths before". So in this, our 15th year in business, things were looking just fine from a business point of view.

But looking back, I wish now that I could have spent more 'quality-time' with Anne, Matthew, Barbara, Peter and Chris...being a more attentive Husband and Dad. Yes, I was there with them most every night and weekend...and seldom missed a school or social function. But often, my mind was a bit elsewhere...thinking through a client or agency problem. And then, after everyone was asleep, I'd grab a carafe of black coffee and a fresh cigar to head upstairs to our study where I'd work through the night. In all this, Anne was our angel, heart, and glue...never complaining and never missing a beat. It was Anne that managed our household and lovingly raised our kids to the wonderful adults they've become. Even though Anne was an RN with her BS Degree from Columbia University, she gave up a Nursing career to become a full-time mother and wife to our family. In that, I'm certain that her job was as fully demanding as mine!

Of course, both Anne and I realized that my crazy routine of over 80 work-hours a week (not counting those 90-minute drives, both into-and-out-of the City each day) couldn't go on forever. And thanks to my "second career" plans, it wouldn't have to! We had already set the date for my agency phase out...with the first step 'semi-retirement', where I'd work from home. And that was now only about 8-years away!

❖   ❖   ❖   ❖

<u>Views I held strongly at age 43</u>—
- The agency was on solid ground and our business strategy was working.
- The tax-deferred profit-sharing plans we had established were on-track to make it financially possible for me to go 'half-time' at age 51...the target date for beginning my "second career".
- We needed to bring in a new partner with the management skills to carry WB&F forward after Bicking and I left the agency.

<u>Negatives I've carried with me</u>—
- I still hadn't finalized my choice of a "second career".
- I wasn't very good at delegating...and was too much a do-it-yourselfer for an agency our size.
- Too large a percentage of our profits were centered in just two accounts...and it was my personal relationships with their top management that kept the accounts secure and our service fees so high.

❖　❖　❖　❖

Nantucket Island

Discovering Nantucket—

For over 50 years, Nantucket Island was our home away from home. So interrupting the chronology of this memoir to give Nantucket its own special section seemed the best way to tell you about the events and decisions that made it so important to us.

We first visited Nantucket in 1970, when a client recommended the place for our family vacation. We were then 34 years old with 3 young children and had never before heard of the place. From the sound of its name, we assumed it was possibly a beach town somewhere in Rhode Island. But a little research told us it was actually a small island in Massachusetts...30-miles out to sea beyond Cape Cod. Getting there would require taking a 3-hour car ferry from Woods Hole, after a 5-hour car trip from home. But my client assured me that we'd love it.

And we certainly did! In fact, Nantucket eventually became our second home...where we'd spend 4-months a year until we were age 86 when Anne's declining health gave us reason to leave the Island for good. That's a full 51-years from that time we first spied the Island and came ashore.

Stepping back in time—

Nantucket back then was not like it is today. But only in one sense...it was not yet discovered by the rich and famous. Property values back then were dirt-cheap. The shops sold only the basics, plus some handmade items. The restaurants offered only good simple fare. The beaches and the town were uncrowded. The Island's remoteness meant that day-trippers were non-existent.

But in all the most important ways, Nantucket is still much the same (at least as of the time of this writing). Back then...as now... it was like stepping back 200-years in time...with Nantucket's whaling-era Town looking much as it did in the mid 1800s. With more than 400 homes and public buildings dating back to the 1700s and 1800s...most from the Quaker and Federal periods, with all their original architectural detail still intact.

The streets in downtown Nantucket are still paved with cobble-stones and the sidewalks with handmade bricks. The shops are tiny and family run, with no chain stores, modern signs, or neon. The two Main Street pharmacies still have soda fountain lunch counters. And the five historic churches still boast their original pipe organs. Everything is real, not fake replicas!

There are no stoplights in Town or anywhere across the Island... more than half of which is conservation land with scrub-oak covered moors and windswept grasses. The landscape looks more like Scotland than mainland America!

Pristine beaches ring most of the Island...which is bathed by the Gulf Stream, giving it its distinctive curved shape and keeping it cooler in the summer and warmer in the winter than the distant mainland. And like some magical Brigadoon, the whole Island is occasionally enveloped in fog...giving it its nickname "The Grey Lady".

Nantucket's Great Harbor was home-port to hundreds of whaling ships that plied the seas across both the Atlantic and Pacific, and to the outer polar reaches...in their unrelenting hunt for great whales. Nantucket whale oil illuminated the streets of London, the Halls of Parliament, the U.S. Capitol, the White House and the homes of America's most prominent families. And Nantucket spermaceti candles were prized over all others because they burned far brighter and smoke-free...earning them a premium price. All this made Nantucket not only the whaling capital of the world...it made it one of the richest communities in all of America!

But Nantucket was a one-industry town!
Nearly 80-percent of Nantucket's population was engaged in the whaling trade—from ship owners, to captains and seamen, to ship outfitters and coopers, to whale oil merchants, to spermaceti candle makers. This worked to great advantage... until almost overnight the whole thing went away. With the discovery of petroleum and the development of kerosene, the world now had a far less expensive and more plentiful way to keep all those oil lamps burning.

The whale oil market quickly collapsed and Nantucket's population plummeted. Hundreds of its beautiful homes and most of its public buildings soon stood empty...with no one to buy them, regardless of price. As such, like some Sleeping Beauty, they were all preserved in time...only to be awakened nearly 100-years later when tourism came to the Island.

In the early 1900s, there were several major attempts by developers to sell vacation home properties on the Island. But all failed due to Nantucket's remoteness and the dozens of competing developments all along the Atlantic coastline. It was not until 1968, when a guy named Walter Beinecke...a summer resident and heir to the S&H Green Stamp fortune...embarked on an enlightened effort to renew and revitalize downtown Nantucket...as a magnet to attract upscale summer vacationers. Finding investors and putting together something he called the "Nantucket Historical Trust", he brought in dozens of craftsmen skilled in historic preservation to rebuild the deteriorating waterfront and restore the old hotels, small restaurants and shops in the surrounding area. All this was in progress as we first landed on Nantucket!

Over the next dozen years we vacationed a number of times in Nantucket, with each visit more delightful than the last. We only opted for Cape Cod or the Jersey Shore when my Agency schedule kept our vacation getaways to a single week. (Getting to and returning from Nantucket would have chewed up two-full days in travel.)

Buying property—
It was another client who led to our decision to buy a summer home in Nantucket. And it had to do with the prevailing tax laws, which at the time made owning a second home a great tax shelter as long as you set it up as a business and rented it out for part of the year. As the owner, you could use the place yourself for up to two-weeks each year, plus any time you spent there for set-up and routine maintenance. All the operating 'net

losses' that you incurred could be deducted from your 'ordinary income'...reducing the taxes that you would otherwise pay on your salary, financial investments, etc. And the property's net losses could be considerable, at least on paper. That's because under the prevailing tax laws...even though you had a positive cash flow from rental income on the property...you could take a sizeable tax deduction for 'depreciation'. My client described it as a "No Brainer!"

Asking around, I learned that several of my other clients were doing the same thing—buying homes or condos at golf resorts, ski resorts, and beach towns in Florida, Hilton Head, Cape Cod and elsewhere. All had a positive cash flow...along with a big reportable tax loss, which saved them considerable amounts in both their Federal and State taxes. Add to that the potential great return-on-investment. Back then, you could buy a property for 15-percent down, get a good mortgage to keep your monthly carrying costs low...and when it ultimately came time to sell it, fully cash in on the property's appreciated value. It was an amazing way to leverage your money! The only risk was if the property actually declined in value...an unlikely event if you picked an attractive property in an attractive location.

All this sounded great, but still I hesitated. Everywhere we went with TAAN or on vacation, I'd squeeze in a little time to check out potential investment properties. Many looked terrific and their on-paper-profits significant. But each time, I'd ask myself—"If the real estate market ever collapsed, would I really want this place as my permanent second home?" The answer was always—"No." That is, until our 1982 vacation trip to Nantucket!

On a rainy day in July, I visited several properties in Nantucket with a local realtor. One place really caught my eye—a charming brand-new Quaker-style 3-bedroom house with a wonderful view. It was in a largely undeveloped part of the Island called "Tom Nevers"... about 5-miles out of Town, and just a mile or so from the historic hamlet of 'Sconset. I loved everything about it!

The realtor and I rushed back into Town to get Anne, so that she could see the place too. She loved it even more than I did!

So in September 1982, we bought the place...and on its quarter-board we named it "Whael". (You do that kind of thing in seafaring Nantucket.) We negotiated a price of $135,000...with 10-percent down and a very affordable $600/month mortgage. The numbers looked good, because our rental income for the upcoming 3-month summer season would likely bring in $9,600. The closing was scheduled for October. And to be ready for rental showings, we realized that we had to fully furnish the place over the upcoming Thanksgiving weekend. We hurriedly drew up our interior design plans and bought everything we needed in New Jersey. We loaded it all into a big rental truck for the long drive and Ferry trip up to the Island.

With all the furnishings now in place, we enjoyed a post-Thanksgiving holiday in Nantucket with the whole family...and a smaller family gathering during Daffodil Weekend the following spring.

And we were especially fortunate in finding a renter who wanted to book "Whael" for an expanded 4-month season.

When our CPA prepared our 1982 tax return the following April he said—*"Whatever you did, do it again!"* So we did. In 1984 we bought a second Nantucket rental property...a new 3-bedroom authentic post-and-beam house on the adjoining lot in Tom Nevers. The price $160,000. So now we could enjoy two-weeks in each of the two properties whenever we wished. And we took advantage of that by flying up for long holiday weekends, often inviting friends to join us. This second house we named "Punch". Not so much because 'Punch' was the name of the famous satirical British Magazine, but because 'Punch' was the name of my favorite cigars!

Two years later we sold "Whael" to buy the far larger "Flying Cloud". My newest business partner, Andy Morris, had asked us to scout out available properties for him during our 1986 Memorial Day weekend on the Island. In checking out places with our realtor, Gloria Grimshaw, we were surprised to see that home prices had risen dramatically, and that houses were being snapped up almost as soon as they were put on the market. At the end of our tour, Gloria said—*"Let me show you one more place that's under construction and not yet on the market. Priced at $380,000, it's bigger than Andy wants, but the house and views are really fantastic."* So just for fun we stopped there.

She hadn't exaggerated! With four bedrooms and two large great rooms, it would be perfect if we ever wanted to host the entire family or even live semi-permanently on the Island.

Its 3-acre lot was the highest spot on all of Nantucket's south shore...providing unobstructed views in every direction. Wow!

Almost immediately, both Gloria and we came up with the same idea...do a "tax-free exchange" by selling one of our other properties to Andy. I called to see if he was interested...giving him a choice of "Punch" or "Whael". He and Patsy his wife opted for "Whael" and the deal was struck. They bought "Whael" for its newly appraised market price of $280,000...more than double the $135,000 we had paid for it just 4-years prior. And there were no capital gain taxes to be paid, because it was a "tax-free exchange".

So after just four years in the Nantucket real estate market, we ended up with two great houses..."Punch" and our newly named "Flying Cloud"... with a combined market value of over $650,000. If you add together our rental income, our income tax savings, and the dramatic rise in Nantucket property values... these two places effectively cost us nothing! Not a penny! And their market value was still climbing!

A few years later, Anne's mother bought an undeveloped 3-acre lot adjoining "Flying Cloud"...not to build on, but as an investment. When she died, we bought the lot from her estate...giving us a combined 6-acre parcel. We also set up a QPRT Trust to eventually gift both properties to the four Warner children... Matt, Barbara, Peter, and Chris.

Timing is everything—
Tax laws do change. And during the Reagan Administration, there were some big changes. Overall tax rates were cut

substantially...but many of the tax deductions were eliminated. Bottom line...you could no longer use a second home as a tax shelter. This stalled the sales of vacation properties in a big way...but not in Nantucket where the real estate boom was continuing.

Even with the tax law changes, our rental property "Punch" continued to be a good investment. And we'd use it occasionally for overflow guests and for WB&F client workshops and seminars...until when we finally decided to sell it in 1995 for $420,000.

"Flying Cloud" was never rented out after its first season. And we spent more and more time there after my planned early-retirement...ultimately averaging four months each year from 1993 until we sold it in 2021. It was truly our second home! All four of our kids and all five of our grandkids summered with us each year in Nantucket. And we made many close friends on the Island...both summer people and year-rounders. I also became vice president of the Tom Nevers Civic Association and served on a number of Town Committees. We were part of the community... and loved it all!

But in July 2021, we finally decided it was time to put "Flying Cloud" and its adjoining lot on the market...and leave Nantucket for good. The principal reason was Anne's seriously declining mobility and other Alzheimer related issues. Also the recognition that we could never enjoy again the things we loved most about Nantucket—the concerts, the lectures, the plays, the festivals, the parties, the clam bakes on the beach, the museums, the many social functions in Town, in 'Sconset, and at our Church. But in a real sense, we had already lost these things—because the Covid Pandemic had canceled them all for the past two years. After calling our friends to tell them we were putting our properties on the market, we were surprised to learn that three of our four closest friends were doing the same thing. We were all about the same age, and had somehow come to the same conclusion. It was time!

It was also a good time from a financial point of view. The real estate market was at its peak...spurred by the Covid-caused exodus from the cities...as offices, schools, and most public events shut down. If you could now 'work-from-home', why not make that home in a truly great and safe place?

Both properties sold quickly for a combined $4,000,000...which went to the Family Trusts we had set up many years before. Good timing, as our kids were nearing their own retirements and still had some College expenses for the grandkids.

It's certainly an understatement to say that our investment in Nantucket real estate worked out really well. At essentially zero cost to us, we had beautiful homes in one of the World's greatest places for almost 40-years...could give our kids and grandkids cost-free vacations with us every year...and could enjoy the best of both world's—the excitement of the New York Area... and the enchantment of historic Nantucket Island.

But lest you think we were somehow financial geniuses to have planned all this, I have two confessions to make—

1. We had absolutely no idea that this remote island would ever enjoy a real estate boom. After all, every attempt over the past 80-years to develop it had failed completely. We just happened to get there before things took off. We bought our first house as a tax shelter...meaning, that we expected it would actually generate a 'paper loss' to save us some taxes. We certainly hoped that it would eventually sell for a little more than we paid for it. But nothing more!

2. Had I not listened very intently to the advice of my clients, we would have never bought a second home back then...yet alone a second home in Nantucket. We had never heard of Nantucket. Knew nothing about tax shelters. The bottom-line moral is this—Glean all the knowledge that you can from others who you know and trust. Do further research on what at face value sounds like a good opportunity. But then hesitate and carefully weigh the pros and cons...the "what happens if"...evaluating whether it is really right for you. But the always critical first step—Listening with an open mind!

So, don't give us too much credit. Five years later and Nantucket would have been totally out of our price range! And many other vacation-home resorts did nowhere near as well after the tax laws changed.

❖ ❖ ❖ ❖

REFLECTIONS
—After 40 years of life
on Nantucket—

While I had given considerable thought to planning for a 'second career' and early-retirement, where we'd live then never entered into my thinking, yet alone into my planning. I just assumed we'd stay put full time in our home in Ridgewood.

And with my targeted departure date from the Agency still a distant five years in the future, we never for a minute viewed "Whael" as a possible place for retirement. It was just a great little summer house...perfect for few weeks on the Island, but not really for much longer. To us, "Whael" was purely a tax-sheltered investment...with the added benefit of giving us a rent-free place to vacation in our favorite vacation spot—Nantucket Island.

That was 1982...and while we loved Nantucket, it was just too remote for longer-term living. There was no TV reception... even the tallest antenna could scarcely pick-up a flickering Boston station. Phone service was unreliable...with connection to the mainland by microwave transmission, not by hard wire.

Internet and cell phone services were non-existent. Travel to and from the Island was difficult and infrequent...requiring a 3-hour ferry ride or a 5-seatter 'puddle jumper' to the Cape. Weather could sock the place in for days at a time...with all ferry and plane service cancelled. Power blackouts were frequent...as the Island's old electrical generators kept failing. Winters were bleak...with few businesses or restaurants open. The small 'Cottage Hospital' was ill equipped for more than the basics.

Hardly a place to consider for longer-term living!

But it's amazing how quickly things can change when the wealthy 'discover' a place.
Within a few short years, Nantucket became fully connected! First came satellite TV...then cable. Then High-speed Internet with fiber optics. Cell towers. Undersea electrical cables linking the Island to the national power grid. Fast ferries that cut travel time to the mainland to under an hour. And later—major airlines providing direct flights to major cities and hubs. And still later—a state-of-the-art hospital directly linked to Boston's 'Mass General' by both Internet and EMS Helicopters.

The influx of wealthy property buyers also brought Nantucket back to its original glory. The whole Island was declared an "Historic District' and strict zoning and construction rules were enforced. In Town, historic homes and their gardens were attentively restored. In the outlying areas, new homes were built ...all true to the designs and materials mandated by the building codes...with required approval by the "Nantucket Historical

Association". The true historic character of Nantucket was not only maintained...it was significantly enhanced!

All this expanded the appeal of Nantucket for us significantly. The Island now became a viable place for us to spend much of the year. Thanks to the Internet and a great Nantucket Airport, we were no longer remote from anywhere in the World. It was just like being home in Ridgewood...except with far more beautiful surroundings, even more to enjoy, and the camaraderie and charm of small town living.

And thankfully, we owned "Flying Cloud"...a perfect place to call home, from mid-June to mid-October for many years!

❖   ❖   ❖   ❖

<u>Views I held strongly when in 1982 we first bought property in Nantucket</u>—

- It was a good investment that would help us reduce our income taxes.
- We now had a great family vacation home, in a place we really loved.
- We'd probably spend no more than two-weeks a year on the Island.
- Nantucket was just too remote to ever become our retirement home...plus, we'd never want to leave the culture and excitement of the New York City Area.

<u>Views I held strongly when we sold our Nantucket properties in 2021—</u>

- It was the smartest investment we ever made…but who knew?
- It made our lives far more fulfilling…the perfect compliment to our everyday lives back home.
- It gave us the opportunity to spend extended time with each of our kids and grandkids…who vacationed separately with us for almost two weeks each year.
- It let us pass along directly to our children the considerable financial gains from the sale…thanks to the Trusts we had set up many years before.
- Though we loved every moment living in Nantucket, we did not leave with sadness…or with a sense of loss. It was wonderful while it lasted. Now it was on to the next chapter in our lives!

❖　❖　❖　❖

Warner, Bicking, Morris & Partners, Inc.

November 5th, 1990—

That was the day we changed the Agency's name to "Warner, Bicking, Morris & Partners, Inc." The change reflected the fact that Andy Morris was now the Agency's senior partner. And the fact that WB&F had become an ESOP company—with all our staffers effectively becoming Agency owners after their first year with us.

Andy had joined WB&F in late 1981 as VP of Account Services... coming to us from the client side, rather than from another ad agency. After our years of working with him while he was VP of Marketing at our client "Ilford, Ltd.", we saw him as the perfect choice to succeed John and me in running the Agency.

Ilford was a major account. Initially, they hired us to help them, against all odds, become a major player in the U.S. photographic market...a market long dominated by Kodak. A venerable British firm, Ilford had excellent products but was virtually unknown in the U.S. And everyone in the U.S. was quite happy with Kodak.

To gain a foothold, Ilford's strategy was to concentrate exclusively on their Black & White photographic products...both film and printing papers. Not only was this a sizeable market, but professional photographers, photojournalists, and serious hobbyists had long considered Black & White as the artistic medium.

Our launch program directly targeted Kodak with provocative headlines and spectacular Black & White photography. The impact was almost immediate, as intrigued photographers tried out Ilford products and found them superior. Photo dealers and photo labs across the country quickly signed-on as Ilford dealers. Working with Andy on all this was a dream! We functioned as a true team.

A few years later Ilford launched a revolutionary color print material called "Cibachrome". The professional and graphic display market quickly embraced it for its dramatic color brilliance and fade resistance. And it opened a whole new world to photo hobbyists...because thanks to its ease of use, they could at long last make beautiful color prints right in their home darkrooms.

Andy saw the full potential. And together we conducted numerous focus groups and ran a major test-market to guide both the pricing strategy and forecast initial and ongoing product demand. It also led to the decision to market the darkroom equipment and supplies as individual items rather than in combined kit form. Working closely with Andy, we designed the packaging and created all the dealer support materials. And launched a major PR blitz that generated dozens of pages of coverage in all the major Photography Magazines.

Our work with Ilford was not only satisfying, it had a huge importance to the Agency in three key ways—

1. It gave us tremendous recognition within the photographic industry. This led to our winning the Yashica and later the Leica camera accounts.
2. It gave John Bicking the renewed joy he was missing in our business. As a serious photographer with his own home darkroom, he became our lead person on the Ilford account. Thanks to Ilford, "the thrill was back" for John!

3. We met the man who would become the next president of WB&F...Andy Morris!

❖   ❖   ❖   ❖

The agency business is a people business. And people come and go. When Ilford's president retired in 1981, a new CEO was dispatched from London. He proved to be nothing like his fine predecessor. Suffice it to say, after a few months during his tenure, we decided to resign the account. In the NY Times article reporting our resignation, I was famously quoted as saying— *"We got into this business to have fun and make money. And with the Ilford account, neither is possible."* I'm told that Ilford's new president wasn't too happy. But even with my admonition, dozens of agencies lined up to pitch the account. The ad business is also that kind of business!

Before resigning the account, we made a very important decision. Throughout all our years working with Ilford, we were always very impressed with Andy Morris. Certainly, for his marketing and management talents, but even more for his fine character. And our relationship with him was terrific. So I suggested to John that Andy was the guy we should bring in to become our "heir apparent". While Andy had no direct agency experience, he had a sterling track record in both marketing and management. He was a seasoned professional businessman, who knew what it takes to run a profitable firm...unlike so many of the "ad guys" who had worked for us over the years. And John—and my—"early retirement "dates were fast approaching. So it was important that we find our successor sooner rather than later.

We broached the subject with Andy and suggested a plan that would give us both the opportunity to see how things worked out. He'd join WB&F as a VP of Account Services...and after a specified time, he'd receive extra bonuses that could be used to buy Agency stock...with the goal of his becoming a full one-third owner by the end of 1987. He accepted our offer and resigned from Ilford. A month later, WB&F resigned the Ilford account.

Right from the start, Andy and I worked together seamlessly. We lived just minutes apart...so we could carpool together, which gave us nearly three hours most days to discuss client programs, our overall business, and just enjoying each others company. And in short order, Anne and I, and Andy and his lovely wife Patsy, all became very good friends. Things were going very well!

❖ ❖ ❖ ❖

An ESOP Company—
ESOP is the acronym for "Employee Stock Ownership Plan"...a government-approved program that provides special benefits to both employees and retiring owners. In short, it lets employees share in the company's long-term growth. They actually own shares in the company through the ESOP. And it lets the retiring owners sell their shares to the ESOP on a capital gains deferred basis. The whole thing is paid for out of company profits in a way similar to WB&F's already existing profit sharing plans.

As with all our other benefit plans, total credit for discovering and implementing the ESOP goes to John Bicking. It effectively provided John, me, and Andy with an in-house buyer for our WB&F shares...the value of which would be determined each year by an independent auditor. And when the auditor's official valuation came in, it frankly surprised us. It was far higher than we would have guessed. (Normally it's just one-times adjusted gross income in the agency business) And it was far in excess of what we could have probably sold the agency for on the open market. (That's because the only real assets that an ad agency has are its accounts and its staff...all or most of which could walk away in just a few weeks.) But in determining WB&F's official stock value, the independent auditor focused primarily on the profitability of the Agency, rather than its income. And since we had an excellent history of profit growth, our valuation was accordingly high.

As John and I began to sell our shares to the ESOP, Andy became the largest single shareholder. He then moved up to become WBM&P president and we changed the Agency's name.

❖ ❖ ❖ ❖

Soon John began his Agency phase-out. He and Marilyn sold their New Jersey home and moved to Moab, Utah. He'd fly back for a few days in the office each month, and while here, stay with Anne and me in Ridgewood.

John was still in full charge of our financial and administrative systems. And he could accomplish that from Moab because he had installed a duplicate of our IBM computer system in his home office there. Our on-site bookkeeper in New York could handle all the routine daily tasks like billing, collections, dispersements, employee time sheets, payroll, etc. from here.

<u>What about me</u>?

I was still on track for early retirement at age 51, but with a little modification. For my "second career" I had decided that the Presidency of the TAAN Network would be a perfect choice. Expanding the Network worldwide. Working directly with Agency owners to help them succeed. Extensive travel opportunities for Anne and me. All this while working from home in New Jersey and Nantucket. And no clients to deal with. I'd be setting my own schedule and priorities.

So in 1987 at age 51, I signed a 10-year agreement to head TAAN. But knowing that I could accomplish all my TAAN duties in an average of 3 days a week, I also accepted John and Andy's request that I stay semi-active in the Agency to manage the important Thomas Publishing account and to help with new business We came up with the following plan—

- In 1987, at age 51...when my TAAN Presidency began...I'd go half-time at WB&F, but remain on full pay. (That was considered fair, because half-time for me meant about 30+ hours a week rather than my former 80+ hours a week.)

- Then in 1992 (2-years after WB&F became WBM&P and an ESOP company), I'd fully retire from the Agency...with 5-years remaining as the President of TAAN.

So after 1992, I played no role in the daily operations of the Agency...and almost never visited the offices. But because John Bicking and I were still minority shareholders with a financial interest in the Agency, I did remain WBM&P Chairman, active only at the Board of Directors level.

This plan let me transition smoothly into my full retirement life...with more than half my time working from home or Nantucket beginning in 1987.

❖ ❖ ❖ ❖

During the mid-1980s, the Agency's focus and character began to change. We had added a Food Division and a large PR department, and many of the new clients were on fixed retainer fees plus expenses. Among these were divisions of major accounts like Lipton, M&M Mars, Kraft, Best Foods and AT&T. Plus many smaller consumer accounts.

The Food Division was headed by Ron Plummer, who I had worked with many years before at McCann-Erickson. Ron had a major reputation in the Food Industry...and had approached us with an opportunity at a time when our own new business efforts were becoming less productive than normal. The large agency where Ron worked was reorganizing and had just decided to drop all their specialty divisions...including the food division that Ron headed. Having Ron join us seemed like a great opportunity for WBM&P to expand our base of business, so we moved ahead. The match worked very well...until it didn't.

We signed lots of accounts, but the margins were slimmer. Coming to us with the traditional agency mindset of "growth above all", Ron and his staff were not used to our "Managing for Profits" philosophy. They were far less concerned about a client's profitability than its marquis value in building the Agency's reputation. In short, our fees were too low and we had to "eat" many of our time charges. And consistently, our staff would "over-service" the account. That was great for the client, but not so good for us!

For example, I wanted to resign the Lipton account because their VP of Marketing delighted in refusing to renegotiate our retainer fee, even as he piled more and more assignments on us that were clearly beyond the scope of our original agreement. He was just that kind of "prick". Ron argued that we needed Lipton at whatever the cost to bring in new accounts. So we kept it, and kept losing money on it.

Years later, I also learned that our PR director told her staff to ignore Andy's direction to better manage their time on their accounts, which were becoming more and more unprofitable. Her reason? *"For the sake of your future careers, it's far more important to get rave reviews from your clients, than to worry about how much Agency management is making."* Clearly, the concept of employee ownership in an ESOP company had not gotten through, despite special staff briefings and off-site seminars!

❖   ❖   ❖   ❖

In spite of all this, Andy was doing an excellent job running the Agency. We were still profitable, but the challenge of maintaining profitability was greater, with just one senior management person at the helm. He had to do everything that a team of three of us had done before!

And then once again, partner problems began to rear their ugly head. As Andy later told me—*"While I was still at Ilford, John and I worked extremely well together. He was always upbeat and we became pretty good friends. But almost from the first day that I joined the Agency, he never gave me a kind word, and increasingly seemed hostile."* And with time, the situation grew only worse.

As I mentioned earlier, John always stayed at my house in Ridgewood during his monthly visits to the Agency. He'd keep me up late, venting his displeasure with the priority of his "payout". Under ESOP rules, a departing employee was entitled to have their vested shares redeemed immediately in cash. That, of course, would reduce the amount of funds currently available to buy more of John's shares. The only solution was to significantly increase short-term profits and put more money into the ESOP...even if that proved longer-term harmful to the Agency's viability...a concern that John clearly no longer shared. As in those earlier days where John no longer spoke to Phil Gisser... forcing me to become their go-between...the same thing was happening again. Things came to a head when John insisted that the ESOP buy all of his...and my...remaining shares before Andy could even begin to start selling his shares. I objected, saying that was never our plan. With that, John officially resigned...

and promptly sued the Agency and Andy Morris, demanding full payment for all his shares.

In settling with John in order to save the Agency, I had to significantly reduce some of my "pay-out" and Andy's never really began.

There were other more personal issues, but John and I never spoke again.

❖　❖　❖　❖

REFLECTIONS
—After nearly 30 years in Advertising—

I loved the Advertising Agency Business and it was very very good to me. It was during a time when the business was considered glamorous...and the so-called Creative Revolution was at its peak. It gave me the opportunity to work with some of the world's leading companies and the thrill of seeing my ideas and creations contribute significantly to their success. And it let me build a professional reputation that led others to trust me and take my advice.

Of course, it was not all a bed of roses. Tremendously long hours. Dealing with some very difficult clients and an often ego-driven creative staff. While always having to closely watch the bottom line to keep the business soundly afloat during the usual "ups and downs" of the agency business.

By taking the advice of my two mentors—Ram Ramsey and Bill Boylhart—I had put enough away to afford early retirement. And thanks to John Bicking, much of it was in tax-deferred form that let it grow with compound interest.

And I was beginning a new chapter in my life as the president of the Transworld Advertising Agency Network…a part-time "second career", where I'd help ad agency owners in the U.S. and beyond make better business decisions. The days of my having to deal with clients and staffers were over!

❖ ❖ ❖ ❖

Views I held strongly at age 51—

- Ram was right! This was the perfect time for me to move on to a "second career"…with reinvigorating new challenges and lots more personal time to enjoy life. (i.e.- "Get a real life.")
- Bill Boylhart was right! By "Managing for Profits" in the Agency…and avoiding an indulgent personal lifestyle… I'd probably have all the financial resources that Anne and I would need for the rest of our lives.
- But to help me make the right decisions moving forward, I would need to assemble a team of trusted legal and financial advisors.

Views I held strongly at age 56—

- Things were working extremely well…just as per planned.
- I loved heading up TAAN, which I could do largely from home and from Nantucket. Our three annual Network Conferences were held in wonderful places, where Anne and I could extend our stay to enjoy new experiences.
- I should reject consulting requests from former clients. That would only draw me back into my old career.

However—I should keep in touch socially with my closest business friends...particularly those at Thomas Publishing Company.

<u>Concerns I carried with me</u>—

- None really. But one never knows the future, so staying alert and flexible are musts.
- My 10-years of heading TAAN will end in 1997, when I'm 61.

  I should start mapping out my options and plans for <u>full retirement</u> soon.

  We could have as long as 30 or 40 years ahead of us if were lucky!

❖   ❖   ❖   ❖

TAAN
The Transworld
Advertising Agency

1987 - 1997—

When I became TAAN President in 1987...I was taking over from my predecessor Jay Tallant in Denver, who took over from Ram Ramsey in San Diego. Both served a 10-year term. As would I. And in each case, for the first five years of their terms, they overlapped their TAAN duties with a phase-out from their Ad Agencies. As would I. So from 1987 until 1993, TAAN's official new address became...*866 United Nations Plaza, NYC.* Then when I fully retired from WBM&P, the official TAAN Headquarters moved to Ridgewood, NJ. But throughout all 10 years, I did most of my TAAN work from home or Nantucket.

I chose TAAN for my "second career" for a number of reasons. I knew how important it had been to me in shaping both my business and personal life, and I wanted to deliver those same benefits to current and new members. Also, the advertising business was changing in terms of both technology and client services, and I wanted to help TAAN Members make more in-formed decisions in adapting to these changes. Beyond that, I loved the close personal relationships that took root between members and their families. As TAAN President, Anne and I would enjoy warm friendships with great people across the U.S., in Canada and Mexico, throughout Europe and Asia, and beyond. And we'd see them often...at our two annual U.S. Con-ferences, at our yearly European Conference, and occasionally in between. Add to that, expanded opportunities for pleasure travel, with the time to extend our stays. And lastly—unlike so many other "second career" options, there was no investment risk. No company to purchase. No start-up business to get off the ground. No infrastructure and inventories to finance. No employees to pay. My only investment would be time...doing things that I loved to do!

❖ ❖ ❖ ❖

TAAN's purpose had remained the same as when I first joined the Network almost 20-years before. It existed to help the owners of a select group of independent, non-competing ad agencies become more successful in their business and personal lives by sharing their knowledge, experiences and ideas. Personal relationships were the key, which made the careful selection of those agencies invited for membership extremely important. Equally important was that all Members attend every Network Conference. For that reason, attendance was compulsory.

Each TAAN Conference was hosted by a Member in their home city or at a resort site of their choosing. Two full days of meetings were typical, with an added day for the Host to conduct a tour showing-off their Agency and the unique features of their Metro Region. There were evening social events and a full Spousal Program for family members who were attending. And in many cases, Members would extend their stays for mini-vacations.

Members could speak freely about their problems, concerns, and share their successes. They'd describe new capabilities and new services that they were adding...with frank details on the good and bad experiences encountered in their implementation. And importantly, they'd get reactions to upcoming important business decisions, to get feedback and helpful input from their peers.

Most all the formal presentations were by TAAN Members and by the TAAN President. And each Conference had one or more invited guest speakers...on key topics ranging from—new business, management succession, mergers and acquisitions, legal challenges, financial strategies, facilities management, etc. Our TAAN attorney and CPA both attended and made presentations. Both specialized in the advertising industry. And in between meetings, there were frequent communications between Members, and from and with TAAN Headquarters.

I've told you all this to give you some idea of my role as TAAN President. Planning and running the Conferences. Alerting the Members to upcoming changes, opportunities and challenges in our business. And for a few, becoming a mentor. For some others when requested...a kind of "Dutch Uncle" providing frank and honest criticism when needed.

Anne would also be directly involved, acting as "First Lady" to the Members and hosting the Spousal Program. TAAN was truly a family affair!

❖ ❖ ❖ ❖

1993—
I was at the halfway point in heading TAAN. Five years completed and five years yet to go. And I was now officially ending my career at WBM&P. Splitting my time between the two for the

past five years had worked out even better than I had hoped. It confirmed that I had indeed made the right decision, while giving me a little flexibility. *(Burning bridges makes it hard if you ever have to retreat!)*. With an overlapping transition, I could enjoy all that I loved from both...while working more and more from home. And now, from this point forward, it would be only TAAN...with the time at last to jump into my long list of favored personal pursuits!

On my last day at WBM&P, I was treated to two surprise farewell parties on the very same day. The first was a luncheon at the iconic "Four Seasons" on Park Avenue, where the owners and top management of Thomas Publishing wished me a festive and very fond send-off...and presented me with a beautiful Cartier watch. Elated and overstuffed, I returned to the Agency only to learn that I was being feted again that very night at the legendary "Lutèce", where Chef André Soltner himself was preparing a special meal for our entire staff. When I arrived, Anne was there along with Barbara and Bill Sullivan who had flown in from LA for the occasion. It was a day and night to remember. With two huge exceptional meals, that I later jokingly called a *"gastronomical-gastrointestinal extravaganza"*. But with hugs and kisses all around, and a few tears, and a two-way outpouring of affection...it was a kindness on my departure that frankly I never expected!

With Barbara and Bill in town, and with me now a free agent, we spent a week of fun and games. Anne selected a ballet and concert, the Sullivan's picked some plays, and I picked "The Big Apple Circus". All were great, but I suddenly had a strange realization. I was just sitting there totally enjoying each per-formance, without constantly thinking about a client need or agency problem. Multi-tasking had always worked for me, but "Wow", this uni-tasking thing was so much better! Fortunately, by retiring early, I now had the rest of my life to enjoy it!

Another realization was my sleep pattern. For the past 20+ years, I'd average 5-hours sleep a night...with some nights less than 2 and then catching up on weekends. I could function extremely well on that little sleep. But now, without work keeping me up until the wee hours, I slept soundly for 7 or 8 hours every night. No problem with insomnia or wakeful dreams. The realization? I was probably half exhausted for the past 20-years and didn't know it. Now I felt as lively as a spring chick. Who knew?

❖   ❖   ❖   ❖

1997—
My final TAAN Meeting was in Maine at an oceanfront resort... and Members and spouses from all around the world attended. It was a special thrill to have our son Peter there for the meet-ing, in his role as a VP at one of our TAAN Member agencies. Things ended with a festive farewell dinner, with surprises for both Anne and me. There were speeches and jokes, gifts galore, and a "This is your Life" binder with photos and letters from TAAN Members current and past. There was laughter and tears, hugs and kisses, and far too much wine. And moving tributes to both Anne and me. Things ended with a departing gift to us both—an all-expenses-paid invitation to be their guests at the following year's TAAN Meeting in Sydney, Australia...with

a holiday extension to New Zealand. (Actual attendance at the business meetings to be optional.)

I, of course, did my usual event closing dinner speech...this time telling them just how much they all meant to Anne and me over these many years. It was an honor and privilege to know them and work with them, as colleagues and friends. This was an easy speech to write, because it came from the heart!

❖　❖　❖　❖

Is a 'Second Career' right for you?—
It was for me. As it was for several of my TAAN friends. Think of it as an option.
You can decide to 'pace yourself' in business...working hard but sensibly for your entire career. Or you can decide to 'frontload' your entire working career into little more than half the time... permitting you to spend the second half of your prime adult life pursuing personal interests...free of time clocks, bosses, clients and the daily grind. Of course, you'll also be free of those nice paychecks you used to receive... making stockpiling your money early critically important.

The decision is yours, and it all depends on which approach best fulfills your temperament and dreams. At age 55, you might have the hunger, energy and enthusiasm to tackle new things. Or you may so love your existing career that you'll want never to leave it. You might prefer normal retirement at age 65 or 70, then kicking back to enjoy the good life. Or you may actually dread retirement. Many big company CEOs are absolutely miserable in retirement, because their whole identity is wrapped up in the power and prestige they once enjoyed.

It also depends on your company and your position in it. Owning your own company gives you the most options. Working in a larger company may pose obstacles to working extra time for extra pay...unless you're so valuable to them that they pay or bonus you extraordinarily well.

Even if you don't like the idea of early retirement, there's a compelling reason to at least prepare for it financially. The future is unknown. While age discrimination is illegal, you could be sacked in a business turndown or failure. Health or other personal issues could emerge. Or you might just get bored with the work you're doing. My point? Early financial planning gives you options you might otherwise not have. Whatever the future holds, your nest egg is there to make life better.

❖　❖　❖　❖

Anne & Jack

Full Retirement...Life's next stage—

Retiring young is fun. No more pressure and all the time to do whatever you want. And there are so many options. So how do you decide? Will you love it, or will you be at odds? It all depends. And that's why planning for your "post-career" life is probably just as important as planning for your "second career".

<u>Think about what you're giving up—</u>
Working fills up at least one-third of your day, and provides you with professional satisfaction and a circle of colleagues and friends...if you're lucky.

Raising a family and running a busy home fills up even more of your day. And while exhausting, it gives you a true sense of purpose that adds meaning to your life...if you're lucky.

<u>The Challenge—</u>
So what happens when your working days are ended...and your kids are grown and on their own? What replaces all that time? And what replaces that sense of accomplishment that you've enjoyed for all these many years? How do you keep the good and not the bad? Keep the satisfactions and sense of purpose... without the toil and all the pressure?

It depends on many factors—your age, your energy, your health, your zest for life, your talents, your hobbies, your ambitions, your savings...and above all—your shared interests with your spouse. (Assuming that you have a spouse.)

Weigh all these factors. Assess your options. Then draft a preliminary plan. You have your whole life ahead of and you're in charge!

If you choose to fully retire after your "second career" has ended ...as I did at age 61...you'll still have maybe 30 years ahead of you. That's a lot of time! Don't wait until after you retire to figure out your future plans. Don't drift along...just taking things day by day and year after year. Map out a working plan. Certainly, you'll modify or change it as you move along...making new decisions as opportunities come your way, and as situations change.

You'll also find that planning well before retirement is fun. It lets you start dreaming about all those wonderful possibilities that lay ahead. And it may inspire you to get a jump on some of them while you're still working.

I mentioned before the importance of shared interests with your spouse. All too often, this is where longer-term issues can occur...especially if one spouse feels dominated by the other, and is almost never given a say in matters big and small. So it's really wise to draw up your "post-career" plans together... to see just how in-sync you are...or aren't...in your hopes and goals for the future. Any divergent or incompatible views can usually be sorted out, if you discover and discuss them at the outset. And while your interests can differ widely, pre-planning can accommodate you both.

I have many retired friends...couples enjoying life to the fullest. They're so active that they jokingly say—"I don't know how we ever had time for work." They do many things together...and do some things on their own. They have a happy and successful retirement, because they have the best of both worlds!

❖ ❖ ❖ ❖

1997 and beyond...for Anne and me—
Long before retirement...during the course of several evenings...Anne and I compared notes describing our ideal future... and how we'd like to spend our new found extra time together. In most big things we were in full agreement. But we discovered some other things that we never realized were of that importance to the other. Good to know them right up front and put them into our plan. (One example was Anne's wish for us to now see her twin sister Barbara and husband Bill at least once a year, whether here, or in LA, or on a trip together.)

In truth, our plan was not that formal...nothing typed up, dated, and signed. Mainly, it was just a shared verbal understanding, with a few notes and some key target dates for major steps like downsizing.

With that, we moved into our retirement as a team. And here's how that went—

❖ ❖ ❖ ❖

Anne and I were blessed with many good friends over the years...friends from school, from business, from TAAN, from the neighborhood, from clubs, and more. But from that very first year when we first met, there was absolutely no one we would rather be with than each other. And now at last, our time together could be unlimited! So we entered retirement with joy. In a sense, we were picking up right at that point where we were newlyweds again...before responsibilities got in the way. Much older, yes. But still happily remembering all those things we loved to do together. And hoping to do them again some day.

That kept us never bored! We shared the same interests and pursued them together—theatre, classical music, lectures, dinner parties, dances, and travel. Each year we'd take two trips overseas, and maybe one or two in the U.S. And we now spent four full months each year at our Nantucket Island home... where our kids and grandkids would join us for their summer vacations.

We each, of course, had many personal interests to keep us on our toes. Literally, in Anne's case...because she still took ballet classes. She was a VP in her local Woman's Club. And she organized and hosted her Nursing School class reunions. Plus lots more, including a great interest in Fine Arts and both British and American history.

In Ridgewood, I was invited to join a great men's group called "The Hobbyists"...with 415 retired guys "of a certain age", and a calendar of activities that could keep you going almost non-stop. Being exercise adverse, I avoided the golf, hiking, bowling and tennis clubs...even shunned the chess, bridge and poker clubs... but became pretty active in the music appreciation, gourmet cooking and a few discussion clubs...and of course all the eating clubs. There were also trips and tours...for members and their spouses. With other Hobbyist couples, Anne & I enjoyed several short and long trips, including cruises on the Queen Mary 2 and Viking Sun. And we attended most all the gala Hobbyist Dinner Dances, where age appropriate music was played. Through the Hobbyists, we saw first hand just how happy and active couples well into their 90s could be. (And widowers too.)

In Nantucket, I was fairly active in local affairs, something I never had time for in New Jersey. For several years I was VP of our area Civic Association. I also started to write the first of what have now become four books. Only one of which has sold more than a few hundred copies. But that doesn't matter. The enjoyment was in the researching, writing, and seeing them published.

Our Catholic Faith was always central to so much of what we thought and did. Anne became a Eucharistic Minister in both Ridgewood and Nantucket...bringing Holy Communion to those in nursing homes and at the altar. Her devotions and readings focused mainly on Mary, the Saints, and the Missions. I sang in the choir in Nantucket and had a particular interest in the writings of Aquinas and other early theologians. We both loved visiting Cathedrals, Abbeys and historic Churches to study their art and iconography. We both loved early Christian music. And of course, we were always faithful Church goers.

Perhaps it's worth noting here, that we both also held the same conservative views...politically, morally, and socially. That helped us see eye-to-eye in resolving those otherwise gray areas.

❖ ❖ ❖ ❖

The year after I finished my TAAN term, the Chairman of Thomas Publishing Company called to invite me to join their Board of Directors. I accepted and it turned out to be a wonderful experience. It kept me involved in business decision-making and gave me a reason to keep up-to-date with the Internet and evolving computer technology...as Thomas was making a full transition from publishing printed directories and magazines to become a major Internet-only platform.

Thomas Publishing Company had been my client at the Agency for a full 25-years...and the client I had always felt closest to. They were best known for their 16-volume *"Thomas Register of American Manufacturers"*...the premier sourcing tool for companies and the government. Family-owned and operated for over 120-years, Thomas was unlike any other company I ever worked with. Enormously successful, its many directories and industrial magazines were represented by over 500 independent advertising sales representatives around the world. Its President and Chairman were first cousins of about my age, and they welcomed and treated me almost as if I were a member of the family. This gave me the opportunity to contribute directly in the corporation's decision-making...and being intimately involved in all aspects of their marketing. And now as a Board Member, we could get back together and continue a relationship that would last for almost 50 years.

We had Board Meetings at least once a month at Thomas's headquarters in NYC. And to my liking, they were very dressy...with dark suits, ties, braces and French cuffs. I loved that, not only because it gave me an excuse to keep sprucing up my wardrobe, but also because I felt that far too often retired old men dropped their standards and started dressing like the homeless. Dressing up not only reinforces your personal dignity, it says that you are still at your peak...and not a 'has been'.

Each January, the Thomas Board met for several days in Bermuda for a planning session and an in-depth review of all the Company's business areas. Anne and other spouses would attend the social functions...as they would at a few gala dinners throughout the year. As a Board Member, I'd also be invited to the annual Thomas Sales Meetings, where I'd see old friends from my days as their ad agency...and get a first hand sense of their progress, plans, and problems.

Thomas was extremely generous to me...providing comprehensive healthcare coverage, substantial fees, a new computer rig, and beautiful gifts throughout the years. I remained on the Thomas Board for 24 years, until the company was sold in 2021. It was always stimulating, always rewarding, always fun.

One piece of advice—If you have a close business relationship... that can ultimately lead to a future Board of Directors appointment during your retirement... definitely maintain it. Yes, there is the potential for extra income...but even more important is that it can keep you intellectually engaged, and provide you with a solid sense of accomplishment. (And maybe an updated wardrobe, too...if you so wish.)

❖ ❖ ❖ ❖

By serving on a Board after retirement, you'll also find that all your years of professional experience will not be ignored or disregarded. One thing that I encountered in retirement…something that I saw as more amusing than upsetting…was that my 'expert' recommendations were now almost always considered worthless. Where once, top executives in major corporations would listen carefully to my recommendations, and in most cases adopt them, now they were not even acknowledged with a "thank you" or a "yea, but…"

One example—An old school chum was about to sell his family business and expressed great concern about the possible reactions of his senior management staff and long-term employees. Having had direct experience with such issues several times in working with TAAN Members, I offered him some proven suggestions. He hardly listened.

Another example—A homeowners group I was part of, had very low member participation, and expressed concern over how to get more people involved. This was right up my experience alley. I suggested a three-phase solution that would cost almost nothing to implement and that should more than double homeowner participation. Their reaction? No one said anything either pro or con. There were no questions. And after a few minutes of silence, the meeting moved on to other topics.

Clearly, I was no longer the "sage"...the person to be listened to and followed. I was just a guy with some personal opinions. No longer the expert with an answer to their prayers!

What changed? In business they hired me because they believed (or hoped) I could solve their problems. And since they paid me 'big bucks' for my expert recommendations, they valued them accordingly. As a retiree, all those trappings as an expert were no longer present. And they weren't paying me. So my recommendations had no particular value.

I found this all very interesting, and saw how some top corporate executives might find things a bit unbearable in retirement. That is...unless they had something new and exciting to engage them. A second career? A new advocacy? A position in Government or Education? Serving on some Corporate Boards? Or like me—some creative pursuits that they valued far more highly than being listened to!

As written in Mark 6:4—"*A prophet in his home town has little honor.*"

❖   ❖   ❖   ❖

The End of an Era—
In 2003, my dear Mother died, just shy of age 102. For the past seven years, she had lived at the Van Dyke Manor nursing home in Ridgewood, where the whole family could visit her frequently. At age 95, she had agreed that it was finally time to leave her lifelong home in Green Island, to be closer to us all. Van Dyke

was the same Ridgewood nursing home where Anne's mother had lived until her death in 1994. Both were wonderful ladies... loving, caring, and always asking how they could help.

❖   ❖   ❖   ❖

Another significant event was the sale of WBM&P to a large Philadelphia ad agency that wanted a larger presence in NYC. The year was 1998...five years after my agency "Farewell Dinner". The acquiring agency was *"Earle Palmer Brown"*. Andy Morris was ready to retire, and the time seemed right to sell the place. After negotiating the sale and managing the transition, Andy and Patsy moved to Colorado...near to two of their children. They also sold their Nantucket property...trading ocean spray for mountain grandeur.

"Warner, Bicking & Fenwick" and its successor "Warner, Bicking, Morris & Partners" had flourished for 34 years...quite a record in the mid-size agency business. And for almost 30 of those years, it had given me a creative outlet and stretched my skills to levels I might have never otherwise foreseen. It had given me true job satisfaction and brought me into close contact with hundreds of truly remarkable men and women. And it provided me and my family with a very comfortable lifestyle, well beyond that of my boyhood dreams.

Do I look back and miss it all? Certainly I did look back to write this memoir...and I remember it all most fondly. But as they say..."Looking back takes your eyes off what's directly ahead of you." I've always felt that way!

❖   ❖   ❖   ❖

Another move—

In 2014, we sold our big Ridgewood home of 45-years and moved to a large single-floor condo in Montvale, NJ. Less than15-minutes away from our old neighborhood, it just made life more convenient. No stairs, no yard work, no maintenance, and a spacious two-car garage with an elevator to our 3rd-floor apartment. Great views, lots of storage space, a clubhouse and pool area for social events. Called "Four Seasons at Ridgemont", it was a 55-plus community that consisted of nine 3-story build-ings, with four-large single-floor apartments on each floor...for a total of 108 units in all. It was brand new, beautifully land-scaped...perfect for our future needs.

We selected "Four Seasons" for its facilities and location, but soon found that our wonderful new neighbors were an even greater asset. We made many new friends here at a time when so many in the old neighborhood were moving permanently away. While almost half our neighbors at "Four Seasons" owned homes in Florida (they were *Snow Birds* spending the winter there and returning north in the spring), Anne and I did almost the opposite...living in Nantucket in the summer and returning home in the fall. But that still gave us enough time in between to become good friends.

❖   ❖   ❖   ❖

2021...Life Interrupted—

You can't know exactly when they will come. Or the form they will take. But unforeseen circumstances and poor health lie just over the horizon for us all.

And they will most assuredly change your life.

The first event was the Covid Pandemic, which pretty much shut down the country for nearly two years...forcing us to cancel almost everything we had planned to do. And far more significant was Anne's failing health.

Some 3-years earlier, Anne had noticed that she was having a little trouble keeping her balance...and more worrisome, that her memory was slipping. After extensive tests, her doctors had determined that it was early-onset Alzheimer's disease. By 2021, she could no longer walk unaided or leave the upstairs level of our Nantucket home. And the long trip to and from the Island was becoming too difficult. That's when we decided to sell the place, no longer to return.

Back home, Anne's condition continued to deteriorate. There was no pain, but increasingly she could no longer do anything unassisted. She remained cheerful, but her cognitive impairment grew significantly. Fortunately, we had caring and competent health aides to assist us. First, two days a week from 9:00 to 5:00. Then ultimately, seven days a week from 9:00 to 7:00.

By 2023 she slept almost full time...whether in bed or in a recliner. She was my "Sleeping Beauty"...and looked just like a little doll. In August 2023, her doctors said she should enter Hospice Care. And it was God's blessing that the *Villa Marie Claire* in Saddle River, NJ was just reopening after a major 3-year renovation...designed to make it the model for future Hospice Care...not only in NJ but throughout the Country. Anne was the first patient to enter this wonderful 10-patient facility.

But she was not there for long. I had hoped it would be many months. But Anne passed away just two weeks later on September 13, 2023...surrounded by all our family. She had completed her "long goodbye" and begun her journey into Heaven.

It had been 65-years earlier when I first told Anne that I wanted to spend the rest of my life with her. And I still will! Because she is still with me...in my mind and in my heart!

❖   ❖   ❖   ❖

2024...Life Goes On—
I'm now 88, and for the first time in my entire life I now live alone. I'm as active as ever...keeping busy with family, friends and several projects...like writing this book. My children are wonderful, calling and seeing me often. And this year alone, I'll be taking three cruises...two with my bachelor sons, Matthew and Christopher, and one with my daughter Barbara and her husband Pat. (Peter has a rain check until next year.) In addition to the "Hobbyists", I now also belong to a similar guys group... "Activities Unlimited"...in another town. They have some wonderful discussion groups, giving me the opportunity to keep yapping. And I've recently joined the "Knights of Columbus" and

the Social Club at my Church. I read a lot. Watch a good movie most nights after the news. Set the alarm at 7:00AM and go to bed around Midnight. So far, my health is just fine. I plan to keep going full time, until it's not!

❖　❖　❖　❖

REFLECTIONS
—After 88 years of living—

I've lived a long and very happy life. That's more than any man should reasonably hope for. All due to a series of decisions... some big and some small...that I'd made along the way.

In this memoir, I've tried to tell you about those decisions...how and why I made them. Not as examples that you might follow, but rather to give you a greater appreciation of how each decision...in turn...alters the course of your journey through life.

Reading the specifics of my own personal life story will no doubt be of special interest to my family and friends. Far less so to others. But hopefully, hearing them will add a little 'flesh and blood' reality to what otherwise might have been a pretty preachy 'how-to' tome.

How good were my decisions? As you've seen, some were fairly bad. But thankfully I had the time to 'save the day' with a better decision that followed.

Without doubt, if I'd made different decisions, things assuredly would have turned out differently. Possibly better. Possibly worse. But definitely not the same. I'll never know. And frankly, I'm all right with that!

❖   ❖   ❖   ❖

A life in full—
In writing this book, I've had the chance to reflect upon my life in full...and all the many decisions that brought me to the place I am today. And necessarily, they've mainly been chronological... from childhood to old age.

But what of the relative importance of these decisions? Which stand out as absolutely critical to my happiness in life? Only three stand out. And they are these—

1. Asking Anne to become my wife...and striving to keep worthy of her love.
2. Choosing Advertising as my career...which gave me creative and professional joy.
3. Retiring Early...to let us live our life to the very fullest.

As I said—What more could any man reasonably hope for?

❖   ❖   ❖   ❖

Summing Up

Decisions—

Life is all about decision-making. Hundreds of them each day.
Most are inconsequential... *what socks to wear?*
Some just moderately so... *should I call him back now or later?*
And some are profoundly important—Decisions re your education, career, spouse, family, finances, health, etc.

It's this latter group that takes all your very best decision-making skills...because taken together they determine your trajectory through life. And as I've tried to illustrate in this memoir, each single major decision leads to another, then another, then another.

Decision-making is really a process...a process composed of three major parts—
1. Recognizing an opportunity that presents itself.
2. Then acting to seize upon that opportunity...or to reject it...or to simply ignore it for now, or perhaps forever.
3. And then assessing the outcome of your actions, to figure out where you go from here.

It all starts with the size and potential of the "opportunity". So the more quality opportunities that you have to choose from the better! But how to get them?
The answer—through your own probing...and, where possible, through the wise-counsel of a Mentor.

❖ ❖ ❖ ❖

Some of those who know me have remarked that I seem to have stumbled into an amazing number of great opportunities. And they ask how do I explain all this good fortune. The best answer I can give them is this—

I'm no one special. Opportunities are out there everywhere. Be a sponge. Keep your eyes, ears and mind open. Be curious. Read a lot. There are thousands of books and articles within easy reach...containing the experience and wisdom of others. Even more important is engaging with others in real in-depth conversations. It's fun to hang out with your buddies talking sports and old times, but that really limits your inputs. A cordial conversation with a stranger can often lead to new insights and ideas...provided that you do the listening.

Finding a Mentor is a far greater challenge...because they'll no doubt be older than you, and be far more accomplished. Perhaps a potential Mentor exists in your own company, or community, or family. And you may spot a potential Mentor speaking at a business, professional or social event, at an educational or alumni event. Or perhaps even as a fellow guest at a wedding. If something they say captures your attention, to the point that you want to know more...then approach them and ask if they'd expand on their comments. Perhaps over coffee, or for a brief chat whenever convenient. You'll find that many accomplished people are more than happy to share a little of their time with a nice and respectful person.

If they agree, and then you find that you'd like to establish a closer and perhaps ongoing relationship...recognize that you'll be asking a lot from your potential Mentor. Their time is valuable and they no doubt have a very busy schedule. Being realistic, they'll probably only agree to help you if they see real potential in you. Or they really like you...or ideally both. So that puts the burden on you. And "friendly conversation" is the medium of exchange. So try to be a good conversationalist, and a very good listener.

A Mentor can obviously make a huge difference in your life... opening your eyes to new opportunities...and providing guidance on how to seize them. Hopefully, you'll meet someone remarkable along the way who is willing to become your Mentor.

But not everyone is 'mentor-quality'. There are lots of people out there who'll suggest this or that for your career or your personal life. Listen respectfully. Who knows when a gem may appear? But recognize that most of these random opinions may not fit in with your aspirations.

The ongoing challenge, of course, is figuring out which of life's many opportunities are right for you. It's not enough that they excite you. Do you have the talent, the energy, the resources, and the will power to pursue them? What are the odds of succeeding? What's the downside? And what is your exit plan if things don't work out? And most importantly, how does this opportunity fit into your longer-term life goals?

❖　❖　❖　❖

Some 'rules-of-thumb' that have worked for me—

Everyone has their own style. What works for me, may not be right for you.

But here are the things that have stood me well over these almost 90 years—

- Try to be kind to others...even if they're rude or nasty.

- Try to work hard for your bosses, your clients, and your company...as long as what they ask you to do is moral and ethical.

- Try to see the humor in life...and share it with others to make their day brighter.

- Try to stay focused on your long-term objectives...making mid-course corrections as you go. But never burning bridges in the process.

- Try to learn as much as you can from knowledgeable and experienced people.

- Try to always stay true to your values...resisting peer pressure to compromise.

- Try to make friends that complete you...playing politics can begin to corrupt you.

- Try to be the best spouse and parent you can be...making

it "about them" rather than "all about you". As they wisely say—"Happy Wife equals Happy Life."

- Try to love life by being a good person. Even if you don't achieve everything you aspire to...remember, "Goodness is its own reward!"

- Remember this basic law of mathematics—'negatives add up to negative results'.

❖　❖　❖　❖

Addenda

1. My Family—The only constant in my life
2. Event Timelines
3. Some of Warner, Bicking & Fenwick's Clients
4. My Mentors and their impact on my life
5. Others that I've asked and listened to
6. Ram Ramsey sayings
7. Favorite family stories—confirming that I'm often quite a dolt!

❖   ❖   ❖   ❖

1. My Family—The only constant in my Life...

Like many, I've been blessed with hundreds of friends and acquaintances over the years...several of whom have had a profound impact on my life. But all pale in comparison with my family...the only constant in my life. These are the ones who've loved me just for being me. Clearly, each deserves their own long section describing all they've said and done. But sadly that's beyond the scope of this memoir with its focus on decision-making. However, these few words here are necessary to acknowledge their importance in my life—

<u>My Mother</u>—Ann Frances Warner. Widowed at 58, she chose to remain in Green Island at our family home until she was 95, when a small stroke required her moving to a nursing home. That brought her to Van Dyke Manor in Ridgewood, where we could all visit her almost daily. As bright and sweet as ever, she was a delight to all who knew her. I never heard her speak an unkind word. She loved us all without reservation. She died on April 25th, 2003, just shy of her 102nd Birthday.

<u>Anne's Mother</u>—Dorothy Duffy Hibbard. No one could wish for a finer mother-in-law than Dorothy. Kind and razor-sharp, with a wry sense of humor, she truly treated me as a son. Widowed at 52, she too spent her final years at Van Dyke Manor...where she died on June 15th, 1994 at age 86.

<u>Barbara and Bill Sullivan</u>—Anne's identical twin Barbara married my oldest friend and college roommate Bill...on September 10th, 1960...just shy of a year after Anne and I were married.

And they've lived in California ever since, raising 4 great sons. Though a continent apart, we've been able to visit and vacation together over the years, until the Covid pandemic and poor health ended that in 2020. But frequent phone calls still keep us in contact. Barbara and Bill are sister and brother to me!

<u>My Children</u>—All four are nearing middle age. And my five grandchildren are now young adults. I love them dearly. Admire them greatly. And thank them for their ongoing kindness to me. I could write a volume on each of my children...as they grew to adulthood and left home. But, that would not do them justice. They're grown men and women now...with their own life views and experiences. So I'd encourage each to begin penning their own memoirs...to capture for themselves and future generations the progression of our Warner Family story. But let me tell you very briefly about each of them, from a proud Father's point of view—

<u>Matthew J. Warner</u>—My oldest son, Matt has his own law practice in Wayne, N.J. Super smart, he amazes us all with his wit and command of historical and current happenings. A voracious reader, he's always fun to be with and stimulating to converse with.

<u>Barbara Warner Sheridan</u>—My next born and only daughter is an amazing woman. Kind, sweet, brilliant and beautiful...she together with her wonderful husband Pat have raised three remarkable children...Patrick, Brendan and Claire...all of whom are embarking on their own careers. Before becoming a full-time Mom, Barbara was an ad agency exec. And Pat's career is in financial broadcasting and journalism.

<u>Peter J. Warner</u>—My next youngest, Peter knows more about more things than anyone I know. Enormously well read and in tune with the culture, he dazzles. After a career in advertising production, Peter is now in hotel management. Peter is Father to two bright and engaging children—Xavier, who has just earned his BS in Computer Science...and "Roxy', who is earning her degree as we speak.

<u>Christopher J. Warner</u>—My youngest son, Chris has made his home and career in Washington, D.C. He is the most widely traveled of all my children. His warm and charismatic charm and conversational brilliance make him a delight to be with. Little wonder that he has become one of D.C.'s favorite bar managers.

As a parent, I can't overstate the joy my children and grandchildren bring me daily. One hears stories of siblings who have cool or fractured relationships. Ours are just the opposite. They keep in touch with each other regularly and have fun getting together. As Anne used to say—*"As parents, we must have done something right!"*

<u>My Dear Anne</u>—
How to describe Anne? "An English-Irish Rose!"
Petite and ladylike...but with a twinkle in her eye and a smile that brightened everyone around her. A 5-foot-2 beauty, with very fair skin, hazel eyes, and dark brown hair (although she did become a blonde in later years.) My guy friends have used words like—"cute" and "pert" and "nifty". Our lady friends say—"sweet" and "bright", "a true friend" and "ageless". She was all of that...and a million times more to me!

For more than 65-years, my sweet Anne was my loving companion in our journey through life. Then on September 13th, 2023...
at age 88 in Hospice at the "Villa Marie Claire"...she closed her
eyes for the very last time. Alzheimer's had finally taken its toll.
There was no pain and she looked like an angel...serene and still
looking at least 20-years younger than her biological age. While
I no longer have her here with me to laugh with and to hold,
the wonderful memories of our life together remain very much
alive in my mind and in my heart. Her smiling face and gentle
laugh will be with me always!

❖   ❖   ❖   ❖

In organizing things from Anne's files, I came across an envelope
with this handwritten note from her on the front—*"My favorite
moral advice."*

Here's what her envelope contained. I include it here because
it reveals the kind of loving wife that Anne always was. And
because it suggests how we found true love and happiness
throughout our long marriage.

Loving well requires surrendering yourself—
*What is the secret of a long and happy marriage? It's when two
loving individuals choose to surrender themselves to each other.
Surrendering their pride and their egos in a pact that makes each
of them their partner's lifelong strength and protector. Devoting
their very existence to each other...without reservation, no matter
the challenge.*

Too many see marriage as some kind of romantic fantasy...an extended Honeymoon of sorts. But that rarely stands up to the test of time. Older and wiser partners see marriage more as an alliance and a commitment on the part of two people, who in spite of differences, temptations and disappointments, stay together and support each other by sheer power of their wills. Real love demands constant effort, a full commitment, serious responsibility and dedicated hard work.

Today's culture tells us that true happiness comes from "putting yourself first". That's a lie! Putting yourself first may provide an ego boost and the short-term euphoria of self-fulfillment. But it robs you of the deeper joy found only in the arms of a lifelong companion, dedicated to your wellbeing now and forever. The one who is always there to console you, heal you, and inspire you. Two people becoming one...bound together in loving devotion to each other.

There's a time for being young and foolish, and a time for growing up. Those who love well know that their commitment cannot be allowed to erode because of their own inconstant moods. It requires maturity and strength to bear discomfort gladly for the sake of one's beloved.

Love is patient. Love helps you be cheerful when you want to complain. Love is staying when you want to leave. Love is offering to help when you want to stay focused on something else. Love is calmly accepting criticism when you know you deserve it. Love is being real enough to accept the truth about yourself.

Love is kind. Love knows the difference between..."selfishness" and "selflessness".

Happiness is loving and being loved in return.

Anne loved me...and taught me how to love!

❖   ❖   ❖   ❖

2. Event Timelines—

<u>Life Events</u>—

Date of Birth-	March 26, 1936
LaSalle Institute-	From 1949-to-1953
Holy Cross-	From 1953-to-1957
Married Anne-	September 19, 1959
Anne passed away-	September 13, 2023

<u>Career History</u>—

Union Carbide-	From 1957-to-1962
McCann-Erickson-	From 1962-to-1964
WB&F-	From 1964-to-1993*
TAAN President-	From 1987-to-1997**
Thomas Publishing-	From 1998-to-2021***

  *Half time from 1987-to-1993/**TAAN Member from 1970-to-1987/
  ***Board of Directors

<u>Primary Residences</u>—

Green Island, NY-	From 1936-to-1953
Holy Cross-	From 1953-to-1957
NYC Apartments-	From 1957-to-1959
Palisade, NJ-	From 1959-to-1961
Washington, Twp-	From 1961-to-1969
Ridgewood, NJ-	From 1969-to-2014
Montvale, NJ...	From 2014-to- date

<u>Nantucket Residences</u>—

First visit to Nantucket-	July 1974
"Whael" 1 Wood Hollow-	From 1982-to1986

DECISIONS

"Punch" 6 Chuck Hollow-   From 1984-to1999

"Flying Cloud" 4 Longwood-   From 1986–to 2021

"2B Longwood Drive...   From 1993-to-2021

❖   ❖   ❖   ❖

3. Some of Warner, Bicking & Fenwick's Clients*—

ABC Radio	Helena Rubinstein	Onkyo Hi-Fi
AT&T	IBM	Oticon Hearing Aids
BASF	Ilford Photo	Pillsbury/Wilton
Bell Canada	Isotopes Incorporated	Pirelli
Best Foods	Journal of Commerce	Revere Ware
Careers, Incorporated	Kraft/Polly-O	Texas Gulf Sulfur
Ciba-Giegy	Leica Cameras	Thomas Publishing Co.
Conover-Mast	Lipton Tea	Ticketron/Teletron
Control Data	McGraw-Hill	Victaulic
Corning	M&M Mars	Yashica Cameras
Fordham University	Mikasa Dinnerware	Zerex Anti-Freeze

*Including "Warner, Bicking, Morris & Partners, Inc." Clients

❖ ❖ ❖ ❖

4. My Mentors...and their impact on my life—

Mentor #1—Brother Anselm
- If I had never met him...I would probably never have left the Albany-Troy Area.
- Never gone to Holy Cross.

Mentor #2—My Classmate's Father
- If I had never met him...I would never have gone into Advertising.
- Made my career in New York City.
- Met my future wife, Anne.

Mentor #3—Ram Ramsey
- If I had never met him...I would never have built as successful a business.
- Had as much fun running an ad agency.
- Sold it to semi-retire at age 51...to start a 'second-career'.
- Become president of the TAAN Network.
- Traveled the world with Anne.

Mentor #4—Bill Boylhart
- If I had never met him...I would never have "Managed for Profits".
- Redirected the agency to provide specialized services to larger accounts.

- Accomplished so much for our clients...with as much personal satisfaction.
- Built as large a 'second-career' and retirement fund.

❖ ❖ ❖ ❖

5. Others that I've asked and listened to—

<u>At the Coast Guard Academy—The Commander</u>
- If I hadn't asked and listened...I would never have made the switch to the NROTC program at Holy Cross.

<u>At Holy Cross—The Lt. Colonel</u>
- If I hadn't asked and listened...I would never have been able to launch my advertising career at age 21.

<u>At the St. Patrick's Day Party in NYC—The Copywriter</u>
- If I hadn't asked and listened...I would never have picked Union Carbide over an ad agency training program to start my career.

<u>At a Client Office—Years Ago</u>
- If I hadn't asked and listened...I would never have vacationed in Nantucket.

<u>At Client Offices—Some Years Later</u>
- If I hadn't asked and listened...I would never have bought property in Nantucket.

<u>Bottom Line</u>—Good decisions often come from— asking ...and then really listening!

❖   ❖   ❖   ❖

6. Ram Ramsey sayings—

(Ram was my mentor and friend. Born in 1914, he was 22-years my senior.
We first met when I was 34 and he was 56.)

"You must retire at your pinnacle."

"You can't just retire...you have to retire to something better... something more interesting."

"You must break your emotional ties to your agency."

"Today brings you one day closer to losing your biggest client... or your oldest client...or your favorite client."

"Remember to plan for yourself while you plan for your agency."

"Planning your own retirement is the most difficult plan you'll ever write. It's one of the few events in life where you're totally in charge."

"You've got to plan your exit well in advance...and you'll probably have to finance it."

"If anyone's greedy, this won't work."

❖　❖　❖　❖

7. Some favorite family stories—
confirming that I'm often quite of a dolt!

Lost at Sea—

We were vacationing on Long Beach Island in NJ and the kids wanted us to go sailing on Barnegat Bay. Though Anne was always a bit fearful of boats, she gave in and we rented a small boat with an outboard motor. About two miles out, the motor died and try as I may I couldn't restart it. The tide was fast going out and we were swiftly drifting toward the channel that would carry us out into the Atlantic Ocean. Though the kids seemed to enjoy this, Anne had panic in her eyes. I reassured her that I was very experienced in all things nautical and had the situation fully in hand.

Harnessing all my Coast Guard and Navy expertise, I stood up in our boat, and waving an oar shouted "Ahoy" to a nearby fisherman in an anchored small boat. I pointed to our motor, pantomimed the problem in several ways. He acknowledged my distress signal and gestured for me to stand by. Then...to my total amazement, he stepped over the side of his boat and walked over to us. It seems, the water was only 3-feet deep! A bit embarrassing for me! And long a family joke. But we survived. Although my reputation as an expert in all things nautical did not.

Pilgrimage—

We had a fairly large collection of Mexican religious folk art, which was on display in our Ridgewood master bedroom. But the one thing missing was a large crucifix for over our bed.

On a business trip to San Diego to visit my friend and mentor Ram Ramsey, I asked him if he knew a place where I could buy something special. He suggested that we take a quick trip to Tijuana, where he knew a shop with a great religious art wood-carver. We drove down to the carver's studio and I picked out a beautiful hand-carved natural-wood crucifix about 30-inches tall. After paying, I asked if he could wrap it. The best he could do was newspaper and twine, but I figured I could probably find a carton in San Diego or maybe get one of those suit boxes that the airlines used to give out to travelers.

No luck in San Diego or at the airport check-in. So I arrived at my departure gate with what looked like a big kite wrapped in a Tijuana newspaper tied with coarse hemp cord. The gate agent said I'd have to "check my kite"...but knowing it would be destroyed in the baggage hold...on impulse I did something a bit bizarre! Tearing away the cord and paper...I held high the crucifix with both hands...and as loud as I could declare it, proclaimed—*"I'm on a religious pilgrimage to New York!!!"* Then I solemnly marched down the ramp and onto the plane.

The stunned gate agents froze and didn't challenge me. Nor did the flight attendants inside the plane. Once aboard I never said a word, but continued to hold high the cross as I proceeded down the aisle. A few passengers blessed themselves, but most just looked confused. Fortunately the plane was only about one-third full, so I could strap my crucifix safely beside me.

What possessed me to do this I can't really explain. But I arrived home with my beautiful crucifix intact. And it still hangs over my bed. Were this today, I would have been jailed...or more probably led away to a psych ward! Friends who know this story are convinced that I have a few screws loose! (Perhaps they are right.)

The Jaguar—

I got this bright idea that I could buy a slightly used classic car for little more than a new Detroit car...and at the time, Detroit cars were having major quality problems as they tried to compete with lower cost Japanese imports. So I checked the classified car ads in the *New York Times,* and found a listing for a Jaguar Mark X at a classic car dealer in Philadelphia. As luck would have it, I had a business meeting in Philadelphia the following week, so I called the dealer to ask about the car and make an appointment.

The car was breathtaking! Beautiful and huge! A silver grey body with a contrasting black roof. Supple grey leather seats. Birdseye maple dashboard and interior trim throughout. Rear seats wide enough to almost seat four...with fold-down desks. And not just one, but two separate gas tanks. As I sat in the driver's seat gripping the steering wheel, I glanced down to see that the lighter was engraved with the word—CIGAR. As a cigar smoker myself, I knew instantly that this car was made for me. In addition to the lighter, it had everything...including an AM/FM radio with a built-in tape deck. (At the time, 8-track tapes were pretty new to America and very few cars were equipped to play them.)

The dealer asked if I was interested in the car, and after a test drive and negotiating the price, I told him I'd take it...subject to an inspection by my mechanic. As we shook hands, the dealer congratulated me—saying that my new Mark X was truly one of a kind in America. I enthusiastically agreed…saying—"It has a CIGAR lighter and even a tape deck!" He added—"It has just about everything!"

My Philadelphia mechanic was a long-time friend of my business partner's brother, Donny Bicking, who lived in the area. After the inspection, Donny called me to say that this car was truly amazing…and that his mechanic was especially impressed that it already had a tape deck, because most foreign cars didn't have them yet. So with the mechanic's thumbs-up, I phoned the dealer and told him I'd take the car and come down by train next Friday afternoon to complete the paper work.

Before boarding my train in NYC's Penn Station, I went into a record shop to buy an 8-track tape for my long drive back home…figuring that I'd lose FM radio reception between Philadelphia and Ridgewood. But I pretty much forgot about the tape until I was at a gas station filling up my new car's two gas tanks. People at the station actually gathered around the car asking questions. It was just that amazing.

Before leaving the gas station, I inserted the tape into its slot just beneath the AM/FM Radio controls. But try as I may, I couldn't figure out which of the many buttons and knobs to push or turn to get it to play. Well, I had to get home and figured I'd work things out after reading the manual.

I arrived home safely. And when Anne and the kids finally saw our new Jaguar…their first glimpse of this magnificent beauty…

they were no doubt duly impressed with my sophistication in the field of classic motorcars. But alas, the next day would reveal that this appearance of expertise could be a tad deceiving.

Early the next morning, I went down to the highway to a place called "Car Tape City". The store wasn't yet busy, so right away I got a seemingly knowledgeable teenage clerk who asked how he could help me. Placing my tape on the counter, I asked—*"Do you know if tape decks in the UK are different than those in the States? For some reason, I can't get this 8-track to play in my car."* He said he didn't think so, but would be most happy to take a look at my tape deck.

We went out to the car and he inserted the tape...which fit perfectly. He pulled it out and peered into the slot...jiggling the little nylon roller glides. Then looking up at me, he proclaimed— *"Sir...The main thing...the main problem...is that your tape deck is actually an ashtray."* I sputtered a bit, saying..."Of course... thank you so very much for your trouble."

I drove home, and Anne and the kids asked—"Did he fix the tape deck?"
My reply—*"Tape deck? What tape deck?"*

Yes, it was missing its ashtray. I guess it didn't have everything!"

My Political Career—

At a TAAN Meeting in Barcelona back in 1977, I came this close to being acclaimed the next president of Spain. Franco had died and the whole country was on edge to pick a new leader. Various political parties marched through the streets. Armored military vehicles stood ready at all the major highway axis points. And uncharacteristically, most all the restaurants and night spots closed down before 11:00PM.

We had just finished our afternoon TAAN meeting when I returned to my hotel room overlooking La Rambla. Stripping down to my tee-shirt, I stepped out onto my sixth-floor balcony to gaze down upon a large group of demonstrators about to pass by my hotel. (I should add that back then I had very long curly black hair, and usually had a big black cigar, either in my mouth or hand.)

As I looked down, someone in the crowd spotted me and yelled out—*"El Presidente!"* Everyone quickly looked up and hundreds of enthusiastic Spaniards began to wave and cheer, as they chanted again and again—*"El Presidente!"*—*"El Presidente!"*—*"El Presidente!"*—*"El Presidente!"*

Buoyed by their enthusiastic acclaim, I acknowledged their call by spreading my arms wide...alternately placing both hands over my heart...and then gesturing again and again with out-stretched arms...waving my big cigar as a baton. This went on for several minutes, as I worked the crowd to show my appreciation for their love. Then two things happened—

A TAAN colleague and his son happened to be passing by. My friend told his son to look up, saying—*"Tim...Remember this moment. That man could well become the next president of Spain."*

But then he realized who that man was. It was me. And he said to his son—*"Never-mind."*

Moments later, someone threw a large plastic garbage bag full of water from the roof, drenching many in the crowd. Instantly, they turned ugly and started screaming for revenge. Quickly, I dropped to my knees, crawled back into the room, and cranked down the metal grate sealing off the balcony. My political career had ended, almost as soon as it had begun!

I never entered politics again!

Little Birds—

Driving through Tuscany, Anne and I decided to stop for Sunday Dinner at a fancy restaurant that looked really popular based on all the luxury cars parked in its lot. And once seated, we were excited to find that they were in the midst of their Porcini Mushroom Festival...and that the Chef's specialty that day was a platter of Mixed Roasted Meats...which we enthusiastically ordered.

When the family-style meat platter came, I was overwhelmed to see that it was topped with four very tiny roasted birds...each not more than an inch in length from their miniature beaks to their little claws.

Could these be the tiny birds that *NY Times* food critic Craig Claiborne made famous when he bid $2,000 in a PBS fund raiser to win—"Dinner for Two Anywhere in the World"? He chose a famous restaurant in the Périgord region of France, specifically

313

to eat the tiny wild birds that fed on the grain spilled over from the cages where the Toulouse geese were force fed to produce foie gras.

Claiborne reported that these tiny bids were such a delicacy, they were best eaten under a tented napkin to hold in their aroma. Well I didn't go so far as covering my head with a napkin, but I slowly devoured all four birds...Anne graciously offering me her share.

I have to admit they were a bit disappointing. Perhaps too over-cooked? And they were fairly crunchy...much like eating a late-in-the-season soft shelled crab. But at least I could say that I was now one of the very few who had the opportunity to savor these tiny birds!

After dinner, as I was paying the bill, I asked the proprietor what they called these tiny birds here in Tuscany? With a slight smile he replied—*"Decorations. And we've never had anyone eat them before!"*
Oops!!!

❖ ❖ ❖ ❖